GOVERNMENT DEFICIT AND FISCAL REFORM IN JAPAN

Research Monographs in Japan-U.S. Business & Economics

series editors
Ryuzo Sato
Rama V. Ramachandran
Stern School of Business
New York University
Kazuo Mino
Kobe University
Japan

Other books published in the series:

Sato and Ramachandran
Conservation Laws and Symmetry: Applications to Economics and Finance

Sato, Ramachandran, and Hori
Organization, Performance, and Equity: Perspectives on the Japanese Economy

Sato, Grivoyannis, Byrne, and Lian
Health Care Systems in Japan and the United States: A Simulation Study and Policy Analysis

Sato and Ramachandran
Symmetry and Economic Invariance: An Introduction

Sato, Ramachandran, and Mino
Global Competition and Integration

Negishi
Developments of International Trade Theory

GOVERNMENT DEFICIT AND FISCAL REFORM IN JAPAN

edited by

Toshihiro Ihori
University of Tokyo and Economics and Social Research Institute

Masakazu Sato
Economics and Social Research Institute

KLUWER ACADEMIC PUBLISHERS
Boston / Dordrecht / London

Distributors for North, Central and South America:
Kluwer Academic Publishers
101 Philip Drive
Assinippi Park
Norwell, Massachusetts 02061 USA
Telephone (781) 871-6600
Fax (781) 681-9045
E-Mail: kluwer@wkap.com

Distributors for all other countries:
Kluwer Academic Publishers Group
Post Office Box 322
3300 AH Dordrecht, THE NETHERLANDS
Telephone 31 786 576 000
Fax 31 786 576 474
E-Mail: services@wkap.nl

Electronic Services < http://www.wkap.nl>

Library of Congress Cataloging-in-Publication Data

Government deficit and fiscal reform in Japan / edited by Toshihiro Ihori, Masakazu Sato.
p. cm. -- (Research monographs in Japan-U.S. business & economics)
Includes index.
ISBN 1-4020-7096-9 (alk. paper)
1. Fiscal policy--Japan. 2. Budget deficits--Japan. I. Ihori, Toshihiro, 1952- II. Sato, Masakazu. III. Series.

HJ1391 .G68 2002
336.3'4'0952--dc21 2002066118

Printed on acid-free paper.
Printed in the United States of America.
The Publisher offers discounts on this book for course use and bulk purchases. For further information, send email to <david.cella@wkap.com>.

Contents

Contributors

TOSHIHIRO IHORI
University of Tokyo and Economic and Social Research Institute

RYUTA RAY KATO
Shiga University

HIDEO NAKANO
Senshu University

TOORU NAKAZATO
Sophia University

TAKERO DOI
Keio University

HIROKI KONDO
Shinshu University

MASAKAZU SATO
Economic and Social Research Institute

Aim of the book

This book presents a theoretical-based comprehensive analysis of economic consequences of government deficits and fiscal reform in Japan. Particular emphasis is directed at developing tools that can be applied to theoretically and empirically clarify essential economic concerns in Japan such as generational incidence of fiscal reform and a growing dependence on government bonds for covering financial deficits. This book evaluates the recent movement of Japanese fiscal reform and government deficit.

We first summarize fiscal policy in 1990s. Then, we investigate the macroeconomic impact of government debt and the sustainability problem. We then discuss benefits and costs of public investment. We also consider the political aspect of fiscal reconstruction movements in Japan. Finally, we investigate the behavior of central government's control on local governments' debt issuance and its effect on the real activities of local governments. This book points out that the long-run structural fiscal reform is more important than the short-run Keynesian fiscal policy in Japan.

Chapter 1

Introduction

1. JAPANESE GOVERNMENT DEFICITS IN THE 1990S

This book presents a theoretically based comprehensive analysis of the economic consequences of government deficits and fiscal reform in Japan. Particular emphasis is directed at developing tools that can be applied to theoretically and empirically clarify essential economic concerns in Japan, such as generational incidence of fiscal reform and a growing dependence on government bonds for covering financial deficits. This book evaluates the recent movements of Japanese fiscal reform and the government deficit

As shown in Table 1, Japan's fiscal situation in the 1990s was the worst of any G7 country, having deteriorated rapidly with the collapse of the 'bubble economy' in 1991 and the deep and prolonged period of economic recession which ensued, and from which recovery has been slow and modest despite the implementation of counter-cyclical policy. In this chapter let us first summarize briefly the recent movement of fiscal deficits and fiscal reform in Japan.

After the "bubble economy" was broken in 1991, natural tax decreases reduced revenue. At the same time the politico-economic pressures for larger expenditure budgets and counter-cyclical packages of fiscal measures intensified. Responding to them, MOF (The Ministry of Finance) employed some measures for stimulating aggregate demand. However, these counter-cyclical Keynesian measures were not so effective, resulting in an increase in the fiscal deficit. The planned bond-dependency rate rose from a low-point of 7.6% in FY 1991 (initial) to 18.7% in FY 1994 (initial). The reality was still worse. The implementation of counter-cyclical fiscal policy through Supplementary-Budgets in-year led to further borrowing still, and the actual bond-dependency ratewas more than 22% in FY 1994.

Table 1. Government deficits / GDP

	1990	1991	1992	1993	1994	1995	1996	1997	1998	1999
Japan	-0.4	-0.7	-2.2	-5.0	-5.4	-6.3	-7.1	-5.8	-8.6	-10.0
USA	-3.7	-4.3	-5.3	-4.3	-3.0	-2.7	-1.8	-0.5	0.5	-0.4
UK	-1.5	-2.8	-6.5	-8.0	-6.8	-5.8	-4.4	-2.0	-0.4	-0.7
Germany	-2.1	-3.3	-2.6	-3.2	-2.4	-3.3	-3.4	-2.6	-2.4	-2.1
France	-1.6	-2.0	-3.9	-5.7	-5.7	-4.9	-4.1	-3.0	-2.9	-2.4
Italy	-11.1	-10.1	-9.6	-9.5	-9.2	-7.7	-6.7	-2.7	-2.6	-2.2
Canada	-4.5	-7.2	-8.0	-7.5	-5.5	-4.3	-2.0	0.9	2.0	2.2

The state of the national finances deteriorated rapidly throughout FY 1995 and FY 1996. MOF was forced to borrow 22.0 trillion to finance a deficit swollen by the large fiscal stimulus in September 1995, resulting in a bond-dependency ratio of 28.2%, its highest level since 1980. In FY 1996 the planned issue of 10.1 trillion of special deficit bonds exceeded all previous experience. Despite the gravity of the fiscal situation the initial budgets for FY 1996 and 1997 nevertheless provided for further increases of expenditure, of 5.8% and 3.0%. Not only were fixed costs for prior commitments rising, those for discretionary expenditures continued to rise as well. The servicing of that debt absorbed more than a fifth of the total General Account Budget. Limiting the latter to a 1.5% ceiling in FY 1997 was claimed by the Government and MOF as a sign of new fiscal austerity.

Tables 1 and 2 summarize fiscal situations of G7 countries in the 1990s. The FY 1998 initial budget was drawn up making utmost efforts to deal with the current economic and financial situation within the framework of the Fiscal Structural Reform Act. According to MOF, fiscal reconstruction was equivalent to the achievement of the three policyobjectives of

(i) the elimination of special balanced bonds

(ii) the reduction of the bond-dependency ratio to reduce fiscal deficits on the path to a balanced budget

(iii) the reduction of the size and servicecosts of the accumulated debt

Table 2. Government spending (per GDP)

	government consumption	government investment	transfer payments	others	total
Japan					
1975	10.0	5.3	7.8	3.6	26.7
1993	9.5	6.5	12.0	5.9	33.9
US					
1975	18.6	2.1	11.1	1.3	33.1
1993	17.1	1.6	13.2	4.2	36.2
UK					
1975	22.0	4.7	9.9	8.6	45.3
1993	22.0	1.8	14.6	6.1	44.6
Germany					
1975	20.5	3.6	17.6	6.6	48.3
1993	17.8	2.2	15.8	12.6	48.4
France					
1975	16.6	3.7	17.4	5.7	43.4
1993	19.3	3.6	23.6	6.3	52.8
Sweden					
1975	23.8	4.3	14.2	5.5	47.8
1993	28.0	3.1	25.2	16.2	72.4

The initial budget for FY 1998 marked the beginning of a new realism in the control of public spending promised in PM Hashimoto's 'Vision' of fiscal structural reform. The Fiscal Structural Reform Act, which was implemented in November 1997, had three targets to be achieved by FY 2003.

(i) the elimination of special balanced bonds

(ii) the reduction of general government debt-GDP ratio to 60%

(iii) the reduction of general government deficit-GDP ratio to 3%

General expenditures were down 1.3% over the FY 1997 initial budget, the largest decline in history. However, in the light of the severe economic and financial situation, The Fiscal Structural Reform Act was revised in May 1998, so that income tax reductions could be easily implemented. Furthermore, since the LDP lost the upper house election in July 1998, new PM Obuchi changed the target of fiscal policy. Namely, further tax reductions and increases in public works were implemented to stimulate aggregate demand, following the traditional Keynesian counter-cyclical policy. The Fiscal Structural Reform Act is not regarded as a legal constraint any more. In FY 1998 the issue of special deficit bonds was 21.7 trillion yen due to several fiscal policy measures. By the end of FY 1999 the accumulated debt was total 327 trillion, equal to 65% of GDP. The deficit on the general government financial balance in FY 1999 was 10.0% of GDP, with a gross debt of over 108%. The inclusion of the surplus on social security reduced that deficit to 7.8%, and even that figure was highest among G7.

In order to evaluate the recent movement of fiscal deficits and fiscal reform in Japan, it would be useful to consider the following points. Why does the government deficit matter? Is it really necessary to reduce fiscal deficits? What would the major benefits be of a successful fiscal reconstruction? How would the private sector evaluate public spending in Japan? How would public investment affect private consumption? This book will address these issues.

2. JAPANESE BUDGET PROCESS

The general account of national government is the basic account of Japan. This paper focuses on the general account. The budget process for any fiscal year T (from April of year T to March of year T+1) in Japan begins about nine months before the start of that year. In July of year T-1 the Ministry of Finance issues a guideline including the ceiling of total budget for each Ministry or government agency. Subject to this guideline, each Ministry submits its budget proposal to the Ministry of Finance (MOF) by the end of August. Then, the budget plan is negotiated between the MOF and other Ministries and government agencies during the fall of year T-1. At the end of December of year T-1, or at the beginning of January of year T, the cabinet approves the tentative government budget plan. Although the details of the plan have to be worked out, the total budget size seldom changes after the cabinet approval.

3. BUDGET POLICY IN JAPAN UNTIL 1990

3.1 Balanced budget policy and rise of fiscal deficits

Traditionally, the Japanese government has followed a balanced budget policy. The roots of this policy lie in a conservative view of 'sound' finance which developed in reaction to the extravagant government spending and inflationary pressures during the wartime period and immediately afterwards. A balanced budget was maintained until 1965, when national bonds were first issued in the postwar period. Although national bonds have been floated periodically since then, fiscal deficits did not pose a serious problem until after the mid-1970s.

The gap between government expenditures and tax revenues, which corresponds roughly to fiscal deficits, began to expand rapidly at the outbreak of the first oil shock in 1973. The situation has worsened since the 1970s.

What are the main causes for the sharp rise of fiscal deficits since 1975? Asako et. al. (1991) and Ishi and Ihori (1992) presented good description of the rise and fall of deficits in 1970s and 1980s in Japan. They interpreted that the increase of deficits in the second half of the 1970s as a combination of several factors. Among these, two factors seem important. First, 1973 is referred to as the year that new social security (welfare) programs were introduced. In the early 1970s, several important institutional reforms were undertaken in the social security system with a slogan, "Construct the welfare state in Japan". The share for the program in the total government spending increased automatically during the 1970s, since it was indexed to inflation. This introduction of social welfare coincided with the rapid inflation of the first oil shock, and a change to low growth, so that the long-run revenue trend was miscalculated. The deficit bonds became necessary. Indeed, the real growth rate declined sharply, from 10 to 5 percent in 1973, and to 3 per cent in 1979 when the second oil shock struck the Japanese economy. These experiences resulted in a sharp reduction of tax revenue growth, which in turn contributed greatly to the increase in fiscal deficits during the early 1980s.

Secondly, at the economic summit of 1978, German and Japan were urged by other western countries, notably the United States, to expand their economies to be a "locomotive" for the rest of the world. To keep this promise, Japan took a very expansionary fiscal policy stance, primarily by increasing public investment. Thus, it seems that fiscal deficits occurred mainly due to an unanticipated temporary increase in fiscal spending.

To sum up, the larger fiscal deficits resulted from the major burst of new spending on social welfare programs in the first half of the 1970s and on public investment in the second half of the 1970s and the lack of tax revenues reflecting the slowdown of economic growth.

3.2 Fiscal reconstruction

Let us summarize how Japanese government's deficits have been reduced in the 1980s. Since the increase in the budget deficit in 1975, deficit reduction has become one of the most important objectives of economic policy. Eliminating fiscal deficits was officially called 'fiscal reconstruction'.

Since 1980 the amount of bond issue reduction has been determined at the beginning of the budget preparation process before any other budgetary decisions are made. In order to strengthen the upper limit imposed on budget requests, since 1982 the principle of zero growth requests (zero ceiling) has been imposed. The economic plan, "The Outlook and Guidelines of the Economy in the 1980's" was formulated in August 1983 and designated deficit reduction as one of the main policy targets to be realized by 1989. The Japanese government gave deficit reduction the utmost priority.

At first, the government and MOF attempted to raise tax revenues in the form of a new VAT, i.e., the "general consumption" tax. Such a strategy, however, was completely frustrated when a tax of this kind was politically rejected in the general election of 1979. Then, from the summer of 1979 onwards, MOF constantly pressured each ministry of the government to hold down expenditures when drawing up the initial budget. Namely, in initial budget guidelines limits were set to restrain increased spending. The ceiling was sharply tightened to 10 per cent in 1980 and was lowered further to zero or negative increases for the last several years.

A further important step was the establishment of the Ad Hoc Council on Administrative Reform (Rincho) in 1981. The task of this council was to review all government activities and to make recommendations necessary for rationalizing the government system. Rincho submitted five reports from July 1981 to March 1983 and recommended a number of important reforms to trim overly expanded portions of the government bureaucracy.

Its major proposals were among others

1. privatization of three major public corporations,
2. cuts in spending on public works
3. reduction of the number of government employees,
4. restraint of social security benefits, and
5. simplification of certification and inspection procedures for manufactured products.

Although some of the proposals have not been executed yet, as the result of such policies, the growth of government expenditure has indeed been restrained. In particular, general government expenditures, excluding debt services, did not grow much from FY 1983 to FY 1986. Under these circumstances, the public spending-GDP ratio decreased continuously in the first half of the 1980s.

Special attention should also be paid to the reforms of several major prior commitments, i.e., the reform of health insurance in 1984 and of the social security system in 1985, which contributed a lot to reducing social welfare spending. The rising trend of fiscal deficits was reversed from around 1980 in terms of the bond dependency ratio (the percentage of bond issues to total expenditures).

Along with severe spending constraints imposed by Rincho to promote the goal of reducing deficits, MOF began to fall back on various small measures to increase tax revenues. MOF did not however pursue major tax reforms that would have greatly altered the basic tax structure until the late 1980s. The value added tax (VAT) was finally introduced in the tax structure in April 1989, after a protracted debate.

3.3 Bubble economy

A substantial amount of natural tax increases were produced from 1986 to 1991. This was mainly due to the outbreak of the "bubble economy", which was one of the most remarkable phenomena in the second half of the 1980s. Excess money, chiefly caused by easy monetary policy, flowed into stock and land markets, producing the abnormal hike in asset prices. During the period 1985-1990, the nominal (real) rate of growth averaged 6.0 (4.8) percent. Stock and land price hikes generated a great amount of tax revenues in the form of corporate tax, security transaction tax, capital gains tax, etc. In fact, natural tax increases for FY 1987-88 reached a peak of nearly 10 percent relative to general expenditures ofthe initial budget.

Such a large amount of natural tax increases was of great help in reducing accumulated deficits, which in turn achieved the target of fiscal reconstruction by 1991. The sharp rise of tax revenues, caused by a bubble phenomenon, can be considered a "windfall". "Windfall" tax increases have played a vital role in achieving the MOF's target in the second half of the 1980s.

4. CONTENTS OF THE BOOK

We first discuss the plausibility of a debt neutrality proposition in Japan in chapter 2. The macroeconomic effect of government debt will be analyzed to investigate the plausibility of debt neutrality. We estimate the private sector consumption function based on the Euler equation and investigate the degree of debt neutrality for the Japanese economy. It seems that the strong version of debt neutrality (Barro's neutrality) is not perfectly valid in Japan. Hence, the government debt has some real effects and a debt burden could be transferred to future generations. It seems, however, that people are concerned with long-run effects of fiscal policy. The private sector would have enough information to know the structure of the government budget constraint. It is plausible to conjecture that behavior in the real world may fall between these extremes: the strong version of Barro's debt neutrality and the simple Keynesian hypothesis. In other words, the weak version of Ricardian neutrality is quite valid in Japan.

Chapter 3 then investigates the tax smoothing hypothesis (TSH) for the Japanese government deficit. The tax smoothing hypothesis developed by Barro (1979) suggests that an optimal tax rule is one which smoothes the tax rate over time. The idea is that tax collections are distorting and thus should be allocated over time for the sake of minimizing the present value of tax collection costs. This chapter tests this implication using annual Japanese fiscal data. Our tests indicate that the TSH provides a good approximation for the movements of Japanese fiscal data series although the TSH may not perfectly explain the whole movement. We also evaluate the relative performance of the actual fiscal deficit by calculating the welfare loss due to the divergence from the TSHpath.

Japan is suffering from large government deficits. This is largely due to a slowdown of economic growth in recent years. When national income does not grow much, tax revenue will not increase either. On the contrary, public spending and transfer payments have been gradually raised due to political pressures of interest groups, resulting in large budget deficits. The question of whether Japan's fiscal policy will be sustainable, in the sense of being consistent with an intertemporal budget constraint, has recently been of much concern.

There have been a few analyses of the sustainability problem of government debt in Japan. The data suggests that government debt in Japan was sustainable up until about 1990. However, as explained in chapter 1, deficits have increased rapidly since 1990. We are not sure if the present fiscal system in Japan is sustainable in the long run. By way of comparison, Bohn (1998) showed that the positive response of the primary surplus to changes in debt in the U. S. suggests that U. S. fiscal policy is satisfying an intertemporal budget constraint.

In chapter 4 we test Bohn's condition using annual Japanese fiscal data. This chapter suggests that Japan has two serious points in terms of Bohn's theoretical framework. First, the Japanese primary surplus is apparently a decreasing function of the debt-GDP ratio since 1990 and hence it does not satisfy Bohn's test. Second, the rate of interest is greater than the growth rate in Japan in 1990s. Hence, it is important to reduce the government deficit in the near future.

Chapter 5 tries to examine the effects of the government deficit and public pension policies on the tax burden at a macroeconomic level, capital accumulation and economic welfare in the transition to an aging Japan, by applying a simulated method in the expanded life cycle growth model.

Both the government debt policies and the public pension policies have not been discussed comprehensively. In Japan, a certain amount of the public pension fund exists, and the effect of the outstanding government debt should be comprehensively discussed in relation to the existing public pension fund, since the outstanding government debt and the public pension fund affect capital accumulation oppositely. Thus, the main aim of this chapter is to comprehensively discuss the effect of the outstanding government debt in the transition to an aging Japan by proposing several government deficit policies as well as the public pension scheme within the simulated overlapping generationsframework.

This chapter concludes as follows: First of all, the outstanding future government deficit in Japan increases the ratio of the burden to GDP, which is defined as the tax burden plus the social security burden. This is because an increase in the amount of the outstanding government deficit is followed by an increase in the tax rate to finance the interest incurred from the outstanding government debt

Secondly, a consumption tax is preferable to a wage tax in order to redeem the outstanding government deficit, since a wage tax has a negative effect on savings, thus resulting in the negative effect on capital accumulation.

Thirdly, when a wage tax is used to redeem the outstanding future government deficit, a scenario to maintain a 110% level of the ratio of the outstanding government deficit to GDP in a steady state is not preferable for all generations. However, when a consumption tax is used, this policy would be preferred by the old generations to the policy under the scenario that the outstanding future government deficit is maintained at a 70% level of the ratio of the debt to GDP in a steady state.

Finally, although the size of the effect of the government debt policy on welfare depends on each generation, a lower level of outstanding government deficit in a steady state is preferred by the future generations. This is because a lower steady state level of the outstanding government deficit is followed by an increase in the tax rate at a relatively earlier stage, and this implies that a relatively lower tax is imposed on the future generations to finance the interest incurred from the smaller amount of the outstanding government debt

Spending on public works has been very high in Japan among developed countries. Economic implications of public spending may be evaluated in two ways; the long-run supply side effect and the short-run demand side effect. In Japan the demand side effect has been regarded as the top priority since fiscal policy has mainly been employed so as to stimulate aggregate demand during recession. However, it is widely recognized that the multiplier effect of public works has become very low in recent years, and hence the efficacy of stimulating aggregate demand by using public works is controversial. The resulting cost is a huge government deficitin the1990s.

In the standard Keynesian framework, public works stimulate the private consumption-saving behavior by generating effective demand. However, the supply side benefit of the public works is irrelevant. On the contrary, in the neoclassical framework where people are concerned with the costs and the supply side benefits of public spending, public works may affect consumption-saving behavior. If public works really produce net benefits in the future, they may stimulate private consumption as well as enhancing economic welfare.

By incorporating the benefits of public spending explicitly into the utility function or the production function, chapter 6 investigates the macroeconomic implications of the long-run supply side effect of public works on public consumption. The evidence tends to suggest that the total level of public capital may be too much in recent years. Hence, a further increase in public works would depress private consumption. On the other hand, it is also true that there may be a shortage of public capital in some areas such as public works in urban areas. If the allocation of public works is appropriately revised, then it could stimulate private consumption and enhance economic welfare.

Many governments including Japan are attempting to return to the balanced budget by raising taxes and/or reducing public spending. One of the most common measures is to introduce or raise a general consumption tax partly because this tax would impose uniform shares of the tax burden on all parties in a nation. This is called the fiscal reconstruction movement. Actually Japan introduced the general consumption tax at 3% in 1989 and raised it to 5% in 1997 during fiscal reconstruction

Chapter 7 investigates the behavior of government deficits and fiscal reconstruction movement in Japan both theoretically and empirically. Because of the serious fiscal situation, it is important to evaluate the recent movement of fiscal reform movement in. In the middle of the 1990s, the Japanese budget deficitwas rapidly increasing.

Fiscal reconstruction usually takes much time and public asset balances change over time. It is thus important to explore the dynamic properties of fiscal reconstruction process from the theoretical point of view. The critical point of formulating the fiscal reconstruction process is to clarify how the existing privileges of interest groups, such as preferential treatments of taxes and/or subsidies, are to be abolished.

Why was fiscal reconstruction unsuccessful in Japan? In order to investigate the movement, we first develop a dynamic framework of a fiscal reconstruction process using dynamic game theory among various interest groups. In the case where (income and consumption) tax revenues collected from all groups may be used for all purposes, an increase in tax revenues leads to an increase in privileges by the same amount, and not to a decrease in the public debt. On the other hand, in the case where some portion of the (consumption) tax revenues is tied with spending for future generations, an increase in revenue leads to a decrease in the public debt as well as an increase in privileges. The distribution of the tax increase, that is, contribution of taxes to reducing public debt, depends on the political leadership of fiscal authorities. We then investigate empirically the relationship between the political leadership and fiscal reconstruction process in the Japanese (national) generalaccount.

The fiscal behaviors of Japanese local governments are the most promising database for drawing inferences as to the effects of balanced budget constraints on budget behaviors. Chapter 8 investigates which local governments are permitted more issuances of local bonds by the central government and borrowed more from the FIL (Fiscal Investment and Loan) funds with lower interest rates. Empirical results of this chapter suggest that the central government permits prefectures whose financial capability index are lower, that is, tax revenues are fewer, to borrow more from the FIL funds. It follows that the central government distributes implicitly interregional transfers from prefectures whose tax revenues are more to prefectures whose tax revenues are less, but private financial institutions lend on higher interest rates to prefectures whose fiscal situation is worse and hence average maturity is shorter.

Chapter 9 tests for the effects of a fiscal index set by the central government, measuring the “tightness” of the local government’s budget constraint. This chapter considers how the balanced budget constraint set by the central government would work to limit deficit financing of local governments in Japan.

Chapter 2

Debt Neutrality

1. RICARDIAN NEUTRALITY

The macroeconomic effect of government debt can be analyzed in several ways. Among others, it is important to investigate the plausibility of debt neutrality in the Japanese economy. There are two types of debt neutrality, Ricardian neutrality and Barro's neutrality. It is useful to distinguish the two neutrality propositions for evaluating the efficacy of fiscal policy; the weak version and the strong version. We have the following proposition as Ricardian neutrality, which is the weak version of debt neutrality

***Proposition** 1*: Ricardian debt neutrality
If debt issuance and taxation for redemption of debt are levied on the same generation, debt policy is not effective and the government deficit is a meaningless policy indicator.

Proposition 1 (Ricardian debt neutrality) means that so long as tax relief due to debt issuance and tax burden of debt redemption occur within the same generation, debt policy is meaningless. The government deficit does not matter. Ricardian debt neutrality implies that the agent is concerned only with the lifetime budget constraint and the period-to-period budget constraint is not relevant. However, this result does not necessarily deny the effectiveness of fiscal policy with respect to intergenerational redistribution. Diamond (1965) showed that national debt can be regarded as a device that is used to redistribute income between the younger and the older generations.

From the theoretical point of view, any intergenerational redistribution that can be supported by debt and taxes can also be supported just with taxes and without debt. It is well recognized that if Ricardian neutrality holds, the government deficit is not a useful policy indicator to summarize fiscal action. As Auerbach and Kotlikoff (1987) and Buiter and Kletzer (1992) stressed, unfunded social security could easily be run as an explicit government debt policy. The government can label its social security receipts from young workers either 'borrowing' or 'taxes'. It can label benefit payments to retired people as either 'principal plus interest payments' on the government's borrowing or 'transfer payments'. The economy's real behavior is not altered by the relabeling. This makes one wary of relying on official government debt numbers as indicators of the government's true policy with respect to intergenerational redistribution.

As is stressed by Kotlikoff (1992), generational accounting is a tool of assessing intergenerational redistribution in such a case. It is based on the government's intertemporal budget constraint, which requires that the government's bill be paid by current or future generations. Fehr and Kotlikoff (1995) showed how changes in generational accounts relate to the generational incidence of fiscal policy. Unfunded social security and huge government deficits in Japan would make future generations worse-off in terms of the generational incidence.

2. BARRO'S NEUTRALITY

Barro (1974) extended the neutrality result of Proposition 1 (Ricardian neutrality) to the strong version of debt neutrality

Proposition 2: Barro's neutrality

Under certain conditions debt policy is meaningless even if taxation for debt redemption is transferred to futuregenerations.

Barro studied the effect of debt policy in the altruism model of overlapping generations. The altruistic model means that households can be represented by a dynasty that would act as though they had an infinite life span. He showed that public intergenerational transfer policy becomes ineffective once we incorporate altruistic bequests into the standard overlapping generations model.

The debt neutrality proposition requires a number of key assumptions about the economic environment and the behavior of economic agents. These assumptions include (1) perfect capital markets with no borrowing constraints on consumers, (2) nondistortionary taxes, (3) full certainty about the path of future taxes, government budget policies, and earnings, and (4) equal planning horizon for private and public sectors. The weak version of Ricardian neutrality needs (1)-(3), while the strong version of Barro's neutrality needs (1)-(4).

Bernheim and Bagwell (1987) showed that if families were interconnected via altruism in complicated networks, any change in relative prices would be completely neutralized. They would completely rob the price system of its ability to allocate resources. This conclusion is simply untenable. It tends to cast serious doubt on the Barro model of altruism. In this sense, the weak version of Ricardian neutrality seems more plausible than the strong version of Barro's neutrality. Therefore, the huge debt is harmful in the sense that it leads to the excessive redistribution from the future generations to the present ones. Therefore, we examine Barro's neutrality. We also consider the welfare implications of public debt by estimating a degree of altruism or neutrality if the perfect version of Barro's neutrality fails.

As we have seen, Barro's neutrality holds in the economy where altruistically linked generations behave as the permanent income hypothesis implies. Therefore, the version of the permanent income hypothesis where public sector's budget constraint is taken into account should be tested.

3. THE MODEL

In this section, following Normandin (1999), we present a model of a small open economy with Blanchard (1985) overlapping generations

The lifetime utility of an individual born at time s is

$$E_t \sum_{\tau=0}^{\infty} \left(\frac{1-p}{1+r} \right)^{\tau} \left(-\frac{1}{2} \right) (C_{t+\tau}^{s} - \overline{C})^2, \tag{1}$$

where $C_{t+\tau}^{s}$ denotes consumption and $(1+r)^{-1}$ denotes discount factor. In Blanchard (1985) perpetual youth model, 1-p denotes the probability of being alive in the next period and p corresponds to the birth rate. However, p can be interpreted as a measure of intergenerational linkages' imperfection. Namely, individuals are altruistic only if p is smaller than the actual birth rate. An individual born at time s faces the following flow budget constraint:

$$B_{t+1}^{s} + F_{t+1}^{s} = \left(\frac{1+r}{1-p} \right) (B_t^{s} + F_t^{s}) + W_t^{s} - C_t^{s} - T_t^{s}, \tag{2}$$

where B_t^s, F_t^s, W_t^s and T_t^s denote government debt, net foreign assets holding, stochastic labor income and lump sum tax respectively. For simplicity, we assume that the labor income and lump sum tax are the same for all generations. Also, $(1+r)$ is the gross return on financial assets, the inverse of which is assumed to be equal to the discount factor.

Deriving the optimum levels of consumption for all generations and summing them up leads to the following aggregate consumption function:

$$C_t = \left(\frac{r+p}{1+r}\right)\left[\left(\frac{1+r}{1-p}\right)(B_t + F_t) + E_t\left\{\sum_{\tau=0}^{\infty}\left(\frac{1-p}{1+r}\right)^{\tau}(W_{t+\tau} - T_{t+\tau})\right\}\right], \quad (3)$$

where C_t, B_t, F_t, W_t and T_t are aggregate consumption, government debt, net foreign assets, labor income and lump sum tax.

The government faces the following flow budget constraint:

$$B_{t+1} = (1+r)B_t + G_t - T_t, \quad (4)$$

where G_t represent the expenditures of the government. Budget deficit is defined as

$$D_t \equiv rB_t + G_t - T_t. \quad (5)$$

With (4) and (5), we get

$$T_{t+\tau} = rB_t + r\sum_{i=0}^{\tau-1} D_{t+i} - D_{t+\tau} + G_{t+\tau}. \quad (6)$$

We assume that there are no installation costs in investments and zero profit condition is satisfied. Consequently, aggregate labor income corresponds to the difference between denoted aggregate output (Y) and aggregate investment (I):

$$W_{t+\tau} = Y_{t+\tau} - I_{t+\tau}. \quad (7)$$

Using (6) and (7), the aggregate consumption function (3) can be rewritten as

$$C_t = \left(\frac{r+p}{1+r}\right)\left[\left(\frac{1+r}{1-p}\right)F_t + \left\{\left(\frac{1+r}{1-p}\right) - r\left(\frac{1+r}{r+p}\right)\right\}B_t + E_t\left[\sum_{\tau=0}^{\infty}\left(\frac{1-p}{1+r}\right)^{\tau}\left\{(Y_{t+\tau} - I_{t+\tau} - G_{t+\tau}) + p\left(\frac{1+r}{r+p}\right)D_{t+\tau}\right\}\right]\right] \quad (8)$$

With positive p, the coefficient of B_t in (8) is larger than zero. It means that the present value of the increases in tax expected in the finite lifetimes of the present generations is smaller than the required level to reimburse B_t. Namely, the gap is postulated to the future generations. Therefore, individuals recognize B_t as their wealth to some degree.

On the other hand, in the case p=0, (8) becomes

$$C_t = r\left[F_t + \left(\frac{1}{1+r}\right)E_t\left\{\sum_{\tau=0}^{\infty}\left(\frac{1}{1+r}\right)^{\tau}(Y_{t+\tau} - I_{t+\tau} - G_{t+\tau})\right\}\right]. \quad (8)'$$

(8)' implies that B_t is not recognized as wealth since it has been accumulated in preparation for future tax increases.

Hence, by estimating the coefficients of B_t in (8), we can investigate the validity of Barro's neutrality hypothesis.

4. EMPIRICAL EVIDENCE

4.1 Traditional approach

Leiderman and Blejer (1990) and Seater (1993) presented a useful survey of empirical evidence on the impact of government budget variables on private consumption and on the debt neutrality hypothesis. Homma et. al. (1984) and Ihori (1989) are empirical studies on debt neutrality in Japan. Ihori, Doi and Kondo (2001) estimate a consumption function and investigate the degree of debt neutrality for the period 1970 I -1998 II.

By assuming static expectation formation we can rewrite (8) as the following:

$$C_t = \left(\frac{r+p}{1+r}\right)\left[\left(\frac{1+r}{1-p}\right)F_t + \left\{\left(\frac{1+r}{1-p}\right) - r\left(\frac{1+r}{r+p}\right)\right\}B_t + \frac{p(1+r)}{(r+p)^2}D_t + \left(\frac{1}{r+p}\right)(Y_t - I_t - G_t)\right] \cdot \quad (9)$$

We set the consumption function for the estimation asthe following:

$$C_t = a_0 + a_1(NNP_t - G_t) + a_2B_t + a_3F_t + u_t \quad (10)$$

From the discussion in the previous section, it is natural to denote by $x=1-a_2/a_3$ the degree of debt neutrality

Table 1 reports the estimates of the OLS in first differences. The coefficient on *B* is positive but smaller than the coefficient on *F*. The degree of debt neutrality is calculated as 66% for the whole sample period. The debt neutrality proposition is more valid in recent years (86%) but not perfectly valid.

Table 1. The estimates of a consumption function

	1970I-1998II	1970I-1983IV	1984I-1998II
constant	-0.004	-0.009	-0.03*
	(-0.52)	(-1.02)	(-1.74)
Y-G	0.62***	0.70***	0.59***
	(62.74)	(38.36)	(59.11)
D	0.04***	0.12***	0.03***
	(3.46)	(4.22)	(2.62)
F	0.11***	0.13*	0.18***
	(2.68)	(1.70)	(2.70)
Adj.R^2	0.98	0.98	0.99
DW	2.11	2.04	1.81
η	65.8%	6.49%	86.0%

Note: *** denotes rejection at the 1% significance level, ** at the 5 % and * at the 10%.

4.2 New approach

In many empirical studies including Homma et al. (1987), Ihori (1989), Ihori, Doi and Kondo (2001), an adaptive or static expectation hypothesis is employed in arranging consumption equation like (8) into a testable equation. However, in the recent empirical researches of the permanent income hypothesis, rational expectation is assumed in deriving testable conditions

(Hall (1978) and Campbell (1987)). This method is employed in the test of debt neutrality by Haug (1990) and Normandin (1999). Normandin (1999) arranges (8) into testable conditions and tests the implied restriction for Canadian and US data following Campbell (1987). In this section, we apply this method for Japanese data.

The current account of the small open economy CA_t is

$$CA_t \equiv rF_t + (Y_t - I_t - G_t) - C_t. \tag{11}$$

Using (11) to substitute C_t in (8) and rearranging it yield

$$CA_t + p\left(\frac{1+r}{1-p}\right)(F_t + B_t) + p\left(\frac{1+r}{r+p}\right)D_t = -E_t\left[\sum_{\tau=1}^{\infty}\left(\frac{1-p}{1+r}\right)^{\tau}\left\{\Delta(Y_{t+\tau} - I_{t+\tau} - G_{t+\tau}) + p\left(\frac{1+r}{r+p}\right)\Delta D_{t+\tau}\right\}\right]. \tag{12}$$

In the case p=0, it becomes

$$CA_t = -E_t\left[\sum_{\tau=1}^{\infty}\left(\frac{1}{1+r}\right)^{\tau}\Delta(Y_{t+\tau} - I_{t+\tau} - G_{t+\tau})\right]. \tag{12'}$$

(12) and (12)' can be employed in testing the neutrality

We consider the followingvector auto regression process:

$$\begin{pmatrix} LHS_{t+1} \\ \Delta Q_{t+1} \\ \Delta D_{t+1} \end{pmatrix} = \begin{bmatrix} a_{11} & a_{12} & a_{13} \\ a_{21} & a_{22} & a_{23} \\ a_{31} & a_{32} & a_{33} \end{bmatrix} \begin{pmatrix} LHS_t \\ \Delta Q_t \\ \Delta D_t \end{pmatrix} + \begin{pmatrix} u_t^1 \\ u_t^2 \\ u_t^3 \end{pmatrix}. \tag{13}$$

In (13), LHS_t corresponds to the left-hand-side of (12) and Q_t corresponds to $Y_t - I_t - G_t$. The setting in (13) allows the possibility that *LHS* signals the future changes in *Q* and/or *D*. Such a possibility arises in the case that individuals have superior information. (13) becomes

$$X_{t+1} = \Gamma X_t + v_t, \tag{13'}$$

with $X_t \equiv (LHS_t \;\; \Delta Q_t \;\; \Delta D_t)', \Gamma \equiv \begin{bmatrix} a_{11} & a_{12} & a_{13} \\ a_{21} & a_{22} & a_{23} \\ a_{31} & a_{32} & a_{33} \end{bmatrix}$ and $v_t \equiv (u_t^1 \;\; u_t^2 \;\; u_t^3)'$.

We specify the restrictions among the factors in (13) in the case (12) holds for $p>0$ and test them. At time t, $X_{t+\tau}$ is expected to be

$$E_t(X_{t+\tau}) = \Gamma^{\tau} X_t .$$

The components in the vector are

$$LHS_t = e_1' X_t ,$$
$$E_t(\Delta Q_{t+\tau}) = e_2' \Gamma^{\tau} X_t ,$$
$$E_t(\Delta D_{t+\tau}) = e_3' \Gamma^{\tau} X_t ,$$

where $e_1=(1\;\;0\;\;0)'$, $e_2=(0\;\;1\;\;0)'$ and $e_3=(0\;\;0\;\;1)'$. Substituting the components in (12) using the expressions above yields the following restrictions:

$$e_1' = -\sum_{\tau=1}^{\infty}\left[e_2' + p\left(\frac{1+r}{r+p}\right)e_3'\right]\left\{\left(\frac{1-p}{1+r}\right)\Gamma\right\}^{\tau}$$
$$= -\left[e_2' + p\left(\frac{1+r}{r+p}\right)e_3'\right]\left[I - \left(\frac{1-p}{1+r}\right)\Gamma\right]^{-1}\left(\frac{1-p}{1+r}\right)\Gamma$$

This can be rewritten as

$$e_1' = \left[e_1' - e_2' - p\left(\frac{1+r}{r+p}\right)e_3'\right]\left(\frac{1-p}{1+r}\right)\Gamma , \qquad (14)$$

which implies that all of the three coefficients in the right hand side of the following expression should be zero:

$$LHS_t - \Delta Q_t - p\left(\frac{1+r}{r+p}\right)\Delta D_t - \left(\frac{1+r}{1-p}\right)LHS_{t-1}$$

$$= \left[\left\{a_{11} - a_{21} - p\left(\frac{1+r}{r+p}\right)a_{31}\right\} - \left(\frac{1+r}{1-p}\right)\right]LHS_{t-1}$$

$$+ \left\{a_{12} - a_{22} - p\left(\frac{1+r}{r+p}\right)a_{32}\right\}\Delta Q_{t-1} + \left\{a_{13} - a_{23} - p\left(\frac{1+r}{r+p}\right)a_{33}\right\}\Delta D_{t-1} + \varepsilon_t \tag{15}$$

These three restrictions will be jointly tested for certain values of p. If the restrictions are rejected for p=0, neutrality fails. If the restrictions are not rejected for p positive but smaller than the birth rate, we can say that each generation, which is not perfectly but to some extent altruistic, does plan consumption based on the permanent income hypothesis

Normandin (1999) test the restrictions implied in (12) for Canadian and US data for several values of p. The restrictions in (12)' ((12) in the case of p=0) are rejected for both countries. However, for Canada, the conditions implied in (12) hold for $0.004 \le p \le 0.034$ at the 1% significant level. For US, they cannot be rejected for $0.001 \le p \le 0.016$ at the 5% significant level. For p around 0.01, the restrictions cannot be rejected even at the 10% significant level.

We test the restrictions implied in (12) for Japanese data. For interest rate r, we choose 1%, 2% and 3%.

The restrictions in (12)' ((12) in the case of p=0) are rejected at the 5% significant level. The results mean that Barro's neutrality does not hold. Thus, we consider whether the conditions implied in (12) hold for $0 < p <$ birth rate. Namely, we test the hypothesis that each generation that is not perfectly but to some degree altruistic chooses a consumption level based on the permanent income hypothesis. Figure 1 presents the yearly birth rate and the death rate. We consider the birth rate as $0.006 \le p \le 0.01$ and compare that with the values of p for which the restrictions in (12) hold.

Figure 2 displays the F-value and the horizontal line corresponding to 5% critical level. The restrictions in (12) cannot be refuted for $0.002 \le p \le 0.09$ at a 2% interest rate and for $0.006 \le p \le 0.08$ at a 3% interest rate. The results for some p values are presented in Table 2.

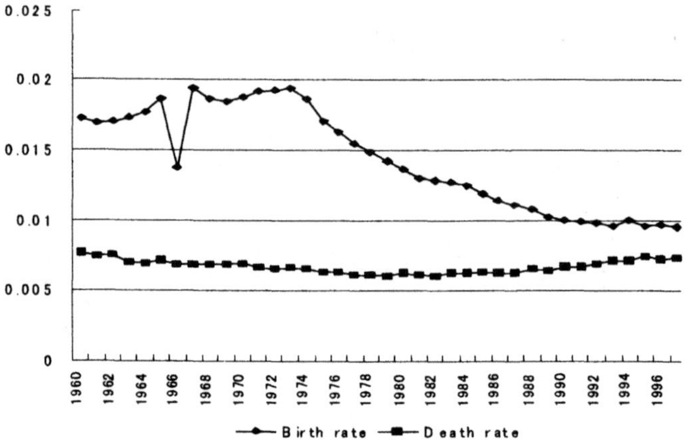

Figure 1. Annual birth and death rates (1976 -1995)

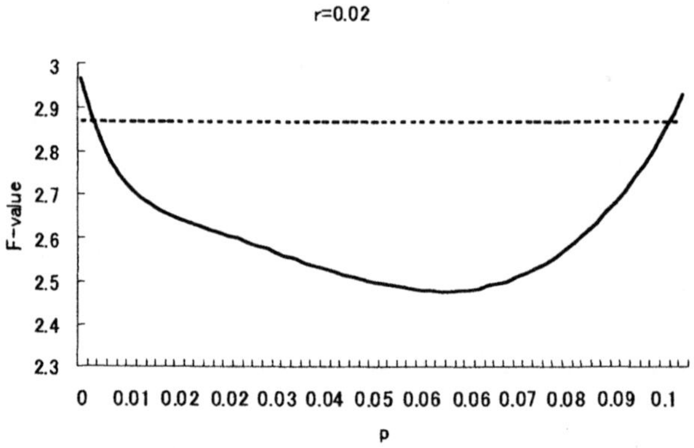

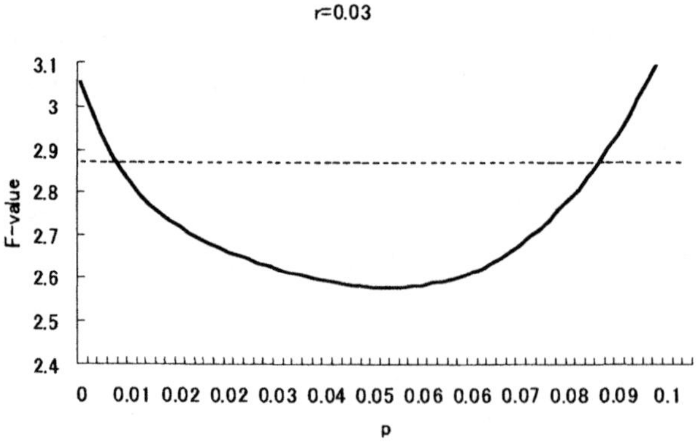

Figure 2. Tests for the restrictions

Table 2. Regression results

$r = 0.02$

p	0	0.005	0.01	0.03	0.05	0.07	0.1
LHS_{t-1}	-0.079	-0.048	-0.029	-0.015	-0.026	-0.046	-0.080
	(-0.874)	(-0.553)	(-0.358)	(-0.220)	(-0.488)	(-0.921)	(-1.788)
ΔQ_{t-1}	0.138	0.129	0.122	0.116	0.123	0.133	0.152
	(0.834)	(0.771)	(0.726)	(0.687)	(0.717)	(0.766)	(0.843)
ΔD_{t-1}	-0.410*	-0.403*	-0.401*	-0.398*	-0.392*	-0.382*	-0.366*
	(-2.522)	(-2.470)	(-2.451)	(-2.406)	(-2.334)	(-2.230)	(-2.058)
F-value	2.966*	2.775	2.694	2.575	2.495	2.502	2.931*
D.W.	2.320	2.322	2.326	2.313	2.271	2.207	2.095
R^2	0.203	0.192	0.188	0.181	0.176	0.177	0.201

$r = 0.03$

p	0	0.005	0.01	0.03	0.05	0.07	0.1
LHS_{t-1}	-0.087	-0.067	-0.052	-0.033	-0.043	-0.061	-0.094*
	(-0.989)	(-0.773)	(-0.625)	(-0.495)	(-0.734)	(-1.190)	(-2.075)
ΔQ_{t-1}	0.138	0.133	0.128	0.121	0.127	0.137	0.155
	(0.834)	(0.795)	(0.761)	(0.716)	(0.738)	(0.783)	(0.857)
ΔD_{t-1}	-0.410*	-0.404*	-0.401*	-0.396*	-0.389*	-0.380*	-0.364*
	(-2.522)	(-2.476)	(-2.449)	(-2.383)	(-2.309)	(-2.206)	(-2.037)
F-value	3.054*	2.891*	2.793	2.636	2.578	2.660	3.261*
D.W.	2.320	2.318	2.317	2.298	2.256	2.192	2.081
R^2	0.207	0.199	0.193	0.184	0.181	0.186	0.218

Notes: Sample period is 1957-1955. *denotes rejection at the 5% significance level.

5. CONCLUSION

We may derive the following implicationsfor fiscal policy in Japan.

First, the strong version of debt neutrality (Barro's neutrality) is not perfectly valid. Hence, the government debt has some real effects and debt burden could be transferred to future generations.

Second, people are concerned with long-run effects of fiscal policy. The private sector would have enough information to know the structure of the government budget constraint.

It is plausible to conjecture that behaviour in the real world may fall between these extremes: the strong version of Barro's debt neutrality and the simple Keynesian hypothesis. In other words, the weak version of Ricardian neutrality is valid.

APPENDIX

All the data we use are from the SNA, "Annual Report on National Accounts" (Economic Planning Agency) and we convert them into real term by using a GDP deflator.

As for T_t and rB_t, we use total receipts and the disbursement minus receipts of property income in income and outlay accounts of general governments respectively. As for D_t, we use balance of saving and investment of general government's capital finance accounts. By using these data, we construct G_t.

We sum up gross fixed capital formation, increase in stocks and net purchases of land of household and non-financial incorporated enterprises defining them as private investment (I_t). As for aggregate output (Y_t), we use gross domestic product. As for CA_t, we calculate net acquisition of financial assets minus net incurrence of foreign liabilities.

As for stock data B_t and F_t, we use general governments net borrowing (stocks of liabilities minus stocks of financial assets) and net foreign financial assets respectively.

REFERENCES

Auerbach, A., and L. Kotlikoff, 1987, *Dynamic Fiscal Policy*, Cambridge: Cambridge University Press.

Barro, R.J., 1974, Are government bonds net wealth? *Journal of Political Economy* 82, 1095-1117.

Bernheim, B.D. and K. Bagwell, 1987, Is everything neutral? *Journal of Political Economy* 96, 308-338.

Blanchard, O. J., 1985, Debt, deficits and finite horizons, *Journal of Political Economy* 93, 223-247.

Buiter, W.H. and K.M. Kletzer, 1992, Government solvency, Ponzi finance and the redundancy and usefulness of public debt, *NBER Working Paper* #4076.

Campbell, J. Y., 1987, Does saving anticipate declining labor income? An alternative test of the permanent income hypothesis, *Econometrica* 55, 1249-1273.

Diamond, P.A., 1965, National debt in a neoclassical growth model, *American Economic Review* 55, 1126-1150.

Fehr, H., and L.K. Kotlikoff, 1995, Generational accounting in general equilibrium, *NBER Working paper* #5090.

Hall, R. E., 1978, Stochastic implications of the life cycle permanent income hypothesis: Theory and evidence, *Journal of Political Economy* 86, 971-987.

Haug, A. A., 1990, Ricardian equivalence, Rational expectations, and the permanent income hypothesis, *Journal of Money, Credit and Banking* 22, 305-326.

Homma, M., H. Abe, N. Atoda, T. Ihori, M. Kandori, and T. Mutoh, 1984, The debt neutrality hypothesis: theoretical and empirical analysis for the Japanese economy, *Economic Analysis*, Economic Planning Agency of Japan (in Japanese).

Ihori, T., 1989, The degree of debt neutrality: some evidence for the Japanese economy, *Economic Studies Quarterly* 40, 66-74.

Ihori, T., T. Doi and H. Kondo, 2001, Japanese fiscal reform: fiscal reconstruction and fiscal policy, *Japan and the World Economy* 13, 351-370.

Kotlikoff, L.J., 1992, *Generational Accounting; Knowing Who Pays, and When, for What We Spend*, The Free Press.

Leiderman, L. and M.I. Blejer, 1990, Modeling and testing Ricardian equivalence, *IMF Staff Papers*, 1-35.

Normandin, M., 1999, Budget deficit persistence and the twin deficits hypothesis, *Journal of International Economics* 49, 171-193.

Seater, J.J., 1993, Ricardian equivalence, *Journal of Economic Literature* 31, 142-190.

Chapter 3

Intertemporal Tax Smoothing and Budget Deficits in Japan: 1957-1997

1. INTRODUCTION

Faced with a prolonged economic downturn in the 1990s, the Japanese government implemented various economic measures, including a series of large-scale public work programs. As a result, the long-term debt outstanding of the national and local governments combined is projected to soar up to 666 trillion yen or about 130% of GDP by the end of FY2001. The steep increases in the government debt give rise to the concern of its future burden and thus fiscal consolidation is now a top priority in medium- and long-term fiscal policy. There is no denying that a rapid increase in government debt might retard economic growth. However, budget deficits also play the role of a cushion that absorbs economic shocks and thus we cannot prematurely conclude a priori that budget deficitsare always undesirable.

The tax smoothing hypothesis (TSH) originated by Barro (1979) suggests that an optimal fiscal rule is to smooth tax rates over time and to finance temporary difference between government expenditure and tax revenue by debt creation. Although the theory of tax smoothing presumes that the debt neutrality theorem (Barro (1974)) is still valid as the first approximation, tax collections are actually distorting and thus tax rates should be smoothed to minimize the distortionary effects of taxation.

Many studies have examined the implication of the TSH, mainly using U.S. data. However, little effort has been directed towards investigating whether the Japanese experience is consistent with the hypothesis. In this paper we will test the TSH for the Japanese budget deficit. We exploit the close analogy between a consumer trying to smooth consumption and a government trying to minimize tax distortion and apply the methodology of Campbell (1987), which is used to test the permanent income hypothesis

The rest of the paper is organized as follows. In Section 2 we show the basic framework of the TSH. Using this framework, we overview previous studies in Section 3. Section 4 contains our test of the TSH, using the data for the period 1957-1997. The last section gives some concluding remarks.

2. A SIMPLE MODEL OF OPTIMAL TAXATION OVER TIME

In this section, we examine the optimal fiscal policy when the government seeks to smooth the time path of taxes associated with the financing of a given path for government expenditure. The objective of the government is to minimize the expected present value of social losses

$$\frac{1}{2}\sum_{\tau=t}^{\infty}(1+r)^{-(\tau-t)}E[\tau_{\tau}^{2}|\Omega_{\tau}]Y_{\tau} \tag{1}$$

subject to the dynamic budget constraint

$$B_{t+1}=(1+r)B_t+G_t-T_t \tag{2}$$

where B_t is the stock of government debt at the beginning of period t, G_t is government expenditure, T_t is tax revenue, τ_t is the tax rate and r is the fixed real interest rate. Ω_t denotes the information set of the government at the beginning of period t. Recursively eliminating future values of the stock of the debt of (1) and assuming that the no Ponzi game constraint

$$\lim_{\tau\to\infty}(1+r)^{-\tau}B_{\tau}=0$$

is satisfied,[1] the intertemporal budget constraint can be written as

$$\sum_{\tau=t}^{\infty}(1+r)^{-(\tau-t)}T_{\tau}=\sum_{\tau=t}^{\infty}(1+r)^{-(\tau-t)}G_{\tau}+(1+r)B_t \tag{3}$$

[1] As shown in Trehan and Walsh (1988), this condition reduces to a test for stationarity of the budget deficits inclusive of interest payments.

or

$$\sum_{\tau=t}^{\infty}[(1+n)/(1+r)]^{(\tau-t)}\tau_{\tau}=\sum_{\tau=t}^{\infty}[(1+n)/(1+r)]^{(\tau-t)}g_{\tau}+(1+r)b_t \qquad (4)$$

where lowercase letters denote corresponding variables expressed as a fraction of GDP and where *n*, the rate of growth of GDP, is assumed to be constant.

Solving the minimization problem (2) subject to the constraint (4) yields the first-order condition

$$E[\tau_{t+i}|\Omega_t]=\tau_t \qquad (5)$$

This states that the optimal tax rate should follow a random walk. Using (4) and (5), we can obtain the optimal tax rate in each period

$$\tau_t=(1-R)\sum_{i=0}^{\infty}R^iE[g_{t+i}|\Omega_t]+(r-n)b_t \qquad (6)$$

where $R\equiv(1+n)/(1+r)$. Therefore taxes are proportional to the present discounted value of government expenditure plus the real interest rate cost of servicing initial debt.[2]

3. REVIEW OF PREVIOUS EMPIRICAL LITERATURE

3.1 Barro (1979)

If the actual tax rates are determined by tax smoothing considerations, the government should issue debt when faced by a temporary decrease in tax revenue or increase in expenditure. Barro (1979) tests this implication by estimating the following equation

[2] Assuming that g_{t+i} be decomposed into deterministic trend, stochastic trend and temporary shock, only the stochastic trend will affect the changes in future tax rates, because deterministic trend is anticipated at present, and current temporary shock, by definition, does not affect the level of future government expenditures.

$$\log(B_{t+1}/B_t) \\ = \alpha_0 + \alpha_1 \pi_t + \alpha_2[P_t(G_t - \bar{G}_t)/B_t] - \alpha_3[\log(Y_t/\bar{Y}_t)(P_t\bar{G}_t + rB_t/\bar{B}_t)] \tag{7}$$

where B_t is the stock of nominal debt at the end of year t, B_t is the average amount of debt outstanding during year t, π_t is the average anticipated rate of inflation during year t, P_t is the average price level for year t, G_t is real government expenditure (aside from interest payments) during year t, Y_t is aggregate real income (GNP) for year t, and Y_t is the level of nominal income during year t.

If the data seems consistent with the TSH, α_2 and α_3 should be positive and should not be significantly different from one. Barro (1979) reports evidence consistent with this hypothesis using U.S. data over the 1922-1976 period.

3.2 Tests using the methodology of Hall (1976)

An alternative approach to test the TSH is to examine the implication that the optimal tax rates should evolve according to a random walk. Under this condition, any variable in the current information set, other than current tax rate, should not help to predict the future tax rates. Barro (1981) tests this implication using U.S. data over the 1884-1979 period and reports that he cannot reject it. By contrast, Sahasakul (1986) found evidence suggesting the opposite. He estimated a version of equation (6)(which adds other variables in the current information set to the right hand side of (6)) and found that these variables could help to predict the future tax rates.

3.3 Tests using the methodology of Campbell (1987)

Huang and Lin (1993) and Ghosh (1995) point out that previous studies have the following shortcomings: 1) the methodology of Barro (1979) and Sahasakul (1986) require empirical pre-decomposition of government spending and aggregate output into permanent and temporary components. To construct the permanent or temporary components, we have to specify the data generating processes (DGP) and thus the validity of the empirical findings may hinge upon the specification of variables or the equation in question. A cleaner test can be accomplished if we can test the hypothesis without any pre-decomposition: 2) even if the tax rates follow a random walk, this does not imply that the government smoothes taxes. The intertemporal budget constraint should also be satisfied under the TSH[3]

Ghosh (1995) proposes an alternative approach that exploits the close analogy between a consumer trying to smooth consumption (as analyzed by Campbell (1987)) and a government trying to minimize tax distortion.

Define the budget surplus (as a fraction of GDP) as

$$SUR_t = \tau_t - g_t - (r-n)b_t \tag{8}$$

If the government sets tax rates by tax smoothing considerations, we can obtain the optimal budget surplus from (6) and (8)

$$SUR_t^* = \sum_{i=1}^{\infty} R^i E[\Delta g_{t+i} | \Omega_t] \tag{9}$$

where $\Delta g_{t+i} = g_{t+i} - g_{t+i-1}$. (9) states the idea that under the TSH the budget surplus should be equal to the present discounted value of future changes in government expenditure and that the budget surplus should Granger-cause future changes in government expenditure. As shown by Campbell (1987), we first estimate a VAR in Δg_t and SUR_t,

$$Z_t = C(L)Z_{t-1} + U_t \tag{10}$$

where

$$Z_t = (\Delta g_t, SUR_t)', \ C(L) = C_0 + C_1 L + \cdots + C_{p-1} L^{p-1}$$

Setting $p=1$ for analytical simplicity,[4] (10) reduces to

$$Z_t = C_0 Z_{t-1} + U_t$$

K-step ahead forecast conditional on the information set Ω_t is,

$$E[Z_{t+k} | \Omega_t] = C^k Z_t$$

Therefore (9) can be written as

[3] Sahasakul (1986) uses the intertemporal budget constraint, but his econometric analysis also requires the empirical decomposition of government spending into permanent and temporary components.

[4] If $p>1$,we can employ the same procedure by stacking equation (10) into a first-order system, as shown in Huang and Lin (1993).

$$SUR_t^* = \sum_{i=1}^{\infty} R^i C_0^i (1,0) Z_t \tag{11}$$
$$= (1,0) RC_0 (I - RC_0)^{-1} Z_t$$

Define

$$RC_0 (I - RC_0)^{-1} \equiv \Lambda = \begin{pmatrix} \lambda_1 & \lambda_2 \\ \lambda_3 & \lambda_4 \end{pmatrix}$$

then we can obtain

$$SUR_t^* = \lambda_1 \Delta g_t + \lambda_2 SUR_t$$

If the TSH is correct, then the coefficient λ_1 should equal zero and $\lambda_2=1$ should equal one. Ghosh (1995) tests this implication using U.S data over the period 1962-1988 and Canadian data over the period 1962-1988 and reports evidence supporting the hypothesis. Huang and Lin (1993) adopt a similar approach and tests the hypothesis using U.S data for the period 1929-1988. Their tests reject the hypothesis for the full sample period but cannot reject it for the post-1947 period.

Another interesting approach is developed by Trehan and Walsh (1988). They showed that if taxes are determined by tax smoothing considerations, tax revenues and government expenditures are cointegrated, assuming that government expenditures are difference stationary. They tested this implication using U.S. data from 1890 to 1986 and reported that the hypothesis of tax smoothing was rejected

3.4 Revenue smoothing

Inflation can be interpreted as a form of taxation, that is a tax on holding money balances, and thus the TSH can be extended to include the theory of optimal collection of seigniorage. Mankiw (1987) shows that, if the government chooses the rates of taxation and inflation to minimize the social cost of raising revenues, the inflation rates as well as tax rates should follow a random walk, and that inflation rates should move together with tax rates. Mankiw (1987) tested this implication (the revenue smoothing hypothesis) using U.S. data over the 1952-1985 period and found a statistically significant positive relationship between inflation and tax rates, a finding consistent with the hypothesis.[5] Poterba and Rotemberg (1990) examine the hypothesis using post-World War II data for a variety of OECD countries and also for the U.S and the U.K, extending the sample period back to 1891 and 1872 respectively. For the U.S. they found evidence supporting the hypothesis. By contrast, for the other countries, only the post-war Japanese data yield a positive relationship between inflation andaxes.

4. ESTIMATION

4.1 Specification and empirical methodology

We examine the TSH for the Japanese government deficit in a VAR framework analyzed by Huang and Lin (1993), following the empirical strategy for the study of linear rational expectations models proposed by Campbell (1987).

As shown in section2, the uniform tax rule

$$E[\tau_{t+i}|\Omega_t] = \tau_t \tag{12}$$

and the intertemporal government budget constraint

$$\sum_{\tau=t}^{\infty}(1+r)^{-(\tau-t)}T_\tau = \sum_{\tau=t}^{\infty}(1+r)^{-(\tau-t)}G_\tau + B_t \tag{13}$$

should be satisfied under the hypothesis. Define the present value of current and future expenditures and tax revenues respectively as

$$\Gamma_t = \sum_{\tau=t}^{\infty}(1+r)^{-(\tau-t)}G_\tau \tag{14}$$

$$\Phi_t = \sum_{\tau=t}^{\infty}(1+r)^{-(\tau-t)}T_\tau \tag{15}$$

(14) implies

$$\ln \Gamma = (1+r)(\Gamma_t - G_t) \tag{16}$$

[5] Assuming that the real interest rates are constant over time, the nominal interest rates should be positively correlated with the tax rates under the TSH. Mankiw (1987) shows that there is a significant positive relation between nominal interest rates and tax rates.

Dividing (16) by Γ_t yields

$$\Gamma_{t+1}/\Gamma_t = (1+r)(1-G_t/\Gamma_t)$$

Taking logarithms on both sides, and using the first-order Taylor's expansion yields

$$\begin{aligned}\ln\Gamma_{t+1}-\ln\Gamma_t &= \ln(1+r)+\ln(1-G_t/\Gamma_t)^{6} \\ &\cong r+k_1+(1-1/\rho)(\ln G_t-\ln\Gamma_t)\end{aligned} \quad (17)$$

where k_1 is a constant and ρ is a constant slightly less than one.[7]
Recursively eliminating future values of Γ_t yields

$$g_0-\psi_0=\sum_{t=1}^{\infty}\rho^t(r-\Delta g_t)+\gamma_1 \quad (18)$$

where g_t=ln G_t, $\Psi_t=\ln\Gamma_t$, $\Delta g_t=g_t-g_{t-1}$ and γ_1 is a constant.

Similar computation using (15) gives the following relationship:

$$t_0-\phi_0=\sum_{t=1}^{\infty}\rho^t(r-\Delta t_t)+\gamma_2 \quad (19)$$

where $t_t=\ln T_t$, $\phi_t=\ln\Phi_t$, $\Delta t_t = t_t - t_{t-1}$ and γ_2 is a constant.[8]
The intertemporal budget constraint can be written as

$$\Phi_0-\Gamma_0=B_0 \quad (20)$$

Dividing (20) by Φ_0, taking logarithms on both sides yields

$$\varphi_0-\phi_0=(1-1/\theta)(b_0-\phi_0)+k_2 \quad (21)$$

where $b_0=\ln B_0$, k_2 is a constant and θ is a constant slightly less than one.[9]

[6] The derivation of equation (17) follows the log-linearization technique developed by Campbell and Mankiw (1989).

[7] ρ can be interpreted as the average value of $1-G/\Gamma$.

[8] We assume that the average value of $1-T/\Phi$ is equal to . for analytical simplicity.

[9] θ can be interpreted as the average value of $1-B/\Phi$.

Using (18), (19) and (21), we can obtain

$$s_t = \sum_{j=1}^{\infty} \rho^j (\Delta g_{t+j} - (1/\theta)\Delta t_{t+j}) \tag{22}$$

where $s_t=(1/\theta)t_t - g_t - ((1-\theta)/\theta)b_t$.

Finally assuming that

$$E[\ln\tau_{t+j}|\Omega_t] = \ln\tau_t$$

holds approximately under the TSH, (22) becomes

$$s_t = E[\sum_{j=1}^{\infty} \rho^j (\Delta g_{t+j} - (1/\theta)\Delta y_{t+j})|\Omega_t] \tag{23}$$

where $y_t = \ln Y_t$ and $\Delta y_t = y_t - y_{t-1}$

(23) postulates that under the TSH a higher (lower) current budget surplus anticipates either a slower (faster) growth of future aggregate income or a faster(slower)growth of future government expenditures.

Now write the multivariate VAR system for s_t, Δg_t and Δy_t as

$$X_t = C(L)X_{t-1} + \mathrm{u}_t \tag{24}$$

where $X_t \equiv (s_t, \Delta g_t, \Delta y_t)$, $C(L) = C_0 + C_1 L + \cdots + C_{p-1}L^{p-1}$ and u_t is a vector white noise process. Stacking the system (24) to form

$$Z_t = AZ_{t-1} + U_t$$

where $Z_t \equiv (s_t, s_{t-P+1}, \Delta g_t, \Delta g_{t-P+1}, \Delta y_t, \Delta y_{t-P+1})$ and noticing that the i-step ahead forecast should satisfy ,

$$E[Z_{t+i}|\Omega_t] = \mathrm{A}^i \mathrm{Z}_t$$

Then (23) can be translated into the following expression

$$\ell' Z_t = \sum_{i=1}^{\infty} (h' - (1/\theta)k')\rho^i A^i Z_t \tag{25}$$

where l, h, k are column vectors with $3p$ elements, all of which are zero except for the first element of l, the p+1st element of h, and $2p$+1st element, which are one.

Since (25) holds for any realization of Z_t, we have

$$\ell' = \sum_{i=1}^{\infty}(h' - (1/\theta)k')\rho^i A^i = (h' - (1/\theta)k')\rho A(I - \rho A)^{-1}$$

or

$$\ell' = (\ell' + h' - (1/\theta)k')\rho A \tag{26}$$

Some calculations using (26) show that the realization of s_{t-i}, Δg_{t-i} and Δy_{t-i} for i=1,2,...,p do not have marginal predictive power over the movement of

$$s_t + \Delta g_t - (1/\theta)\Delta y_t - (1/\rho)s_{t-1}$$

Thus we can test the TSH by estimating the following equation:

$$\begin{aligned} & s_t + \Delta g_t - (1/\theta)\Delta y_t - (1/\rho)s_{t-1} \\ & = a_0 + \sum_{i=1}^{p} a_{1i}\, s_{t-i} + \sum_{i=1}^{p} a_{2i}\, \Delta g_{t-i} + \sum_{i=1}^{p} a_{3i}\, \Delta y_{t-i} \end{aligned} \tag{27}$$

If the data seems consistent with the hypothesis, α_1, α_2, α_3 should equal zero for all i.

4.2 Tests of the TSH

We conduct the analysis outlined above for the Japanese data from 1955 to 1997. The data on tax revenues, government expenditures, government bond issues and national debt services are taken from Zaisei Tokei published by the Ministry of Finance; the data on public debt outstanding are from Kokusai Tokei Nenpo published by the Ministry of Finance; the data on GDP and implicit GDP deflator are from the Annual Report on National Accounts. All data are annual series and deflated by the implicit GDP deflator for the sake of constructing their real data series. The variable T_t is constructed as total revenues minus government bond issues; G_t is constructed as government expenditures minus interest payments on debt. To conduct the tests, the values for ρ and θ must be specified. Setting various values for ρ and θ, we have found that the test results are not sensitive to the values chosen and thus reported results for (ρ, θ)= (0.95,0.95), (0.95,0.99), (0.99,0.95) and (0.99,0.99).

Table1. Tests of the TSH

variable	(1) Ω=0.95 ρ=0.95	(2) Ω=0.95 ρ=0.99	(3) Ω=0.99 ρ=0.95	(4) Ω=0.99 ρ=0.99
(1957-1997)				
$S(t\text{-}1)$	-0.239	-0.197	-0.238	-0.195
	(-4.016)	(-3.302)	(-4.219)	(-3.464)
$\Delta g(t\text{-}1)$	-0.213	-0.213	-0.241	-0.241
	(-0.897)	(-0.897)	(-0.986)	(-0.986)
$\Delta y(t\text{-}1)$	1.119	1.119	0.909	0.909
	(2.427)	(2.427)	(2.146)	(2.146)
Wald statistics	16.149	11.234	17.933	12.548
	(0.001)	(0.011)	(0.000)	(0.006)
(1965-1997)				
$S(t\text{-}1)$	-0.264	-0.222	-0.234	-0.191
	(-3.247)	(-2.724)	(-3.186)	(-2.607)
$\Delta g(t\text{-}1)$	-0.142	-0.142	-0.147	-0.147
	(-0.436)	(-0.436)	(-0.434)	(-0.434)
$\Delta y(t\text{-}1)$	0.959	0.959	0.782	0.782
	(1.780)	(1.780)	(1.519)	(1.519)
Wald statistics	12.197	8.810	12.773	9.119
	(0.007)	(0.032)	(0.005)	(0.028)

Notes)
1.In parentheses below each coefficient are t-statistics constructed by using heteroscedastic-consistent standard errors.
2.The Wald statistics are used to test the hypothesis that all regression coefficients except the constant are zero. In parentheses below each Wald statistic are p-values.

The upper panel of Table 1 gives the results for the period 1957-1997. The coefficients for s_{t-1} and Δy_{t-1} are significantly different from zero. The Wald statistics which measures the joint predictive power of s_{t-1}, Δg_{t-1}, Δy_{t-1} over the dependent variable shows that the implications of the TSH are rejected.[10]

[10] The Schwarz Bayes information criteria are used to choose the appropriate order p for the VAR. The estimating results are similar for p=2 or p=3.

The Japanese government strictly followed a balanced budget policy and thus government bonds were not issued up to 1965. To check whether the results do not depend on the sample period chosen, we estimate the equation for the period 1965-1997. As shown in the lower panel of Table 1, the resulting estimates also reject the TSH.

4.3 Derivation of the optimal path

We evaluate the performance of the TSH by comparing the actual budget surplus with the optimal one under the TSH, which can be predicted by the model.

Using (25) and (26), the optimal budget surplus can be written as

$$s^*_t = \ell' Z_t = (\ell' + h' - (1/\theta)k')\rho A Z_t \tag{28}$$

Therefore, we can construct s^* by estimating the VAR system (equation (24)). Figure 1 plots the actual surplus and the optimal one (as a fraction of GDP) using s and s^*.[11] The actual surplus is slightly higher than the optimal one up to 1964 and thus the actual tax rates were higher than the optimal rates. Deviation between the actual surplus and the optimal one became small in the second half of the 1960s and in the early 1970s. However, the actual surplus was below the optimal one by 1% of GDP due to a slowdown in economy after the first oil shock, suggesting that the amount of government bonds issued in the second half of the 1970s and in the early 1980s was more than the optimal level. The reason why the government failed to raise tax rates to the optimal level is that the government misread the growth potential, which seemed to have had a structural break around 1974, and failed to respond promptly to the shock, as pointed out by Asako, Ito and Sakamoto (1991), although the rise of deficits was partly due to the intended fiscal stimulus. In the second half of 1980s and in the first half of 1990s, deviation from the optimal path was small. Recently, the deviation has become large due to a temporary tax cut for 1998 and a "permanent" tax cut for1999.

[11] We can calculate the optimal primary surplus under the TSH using the optimal tax revenue $T^*_T = T_t \exp[\Omega(s^*_t - s_t)]$

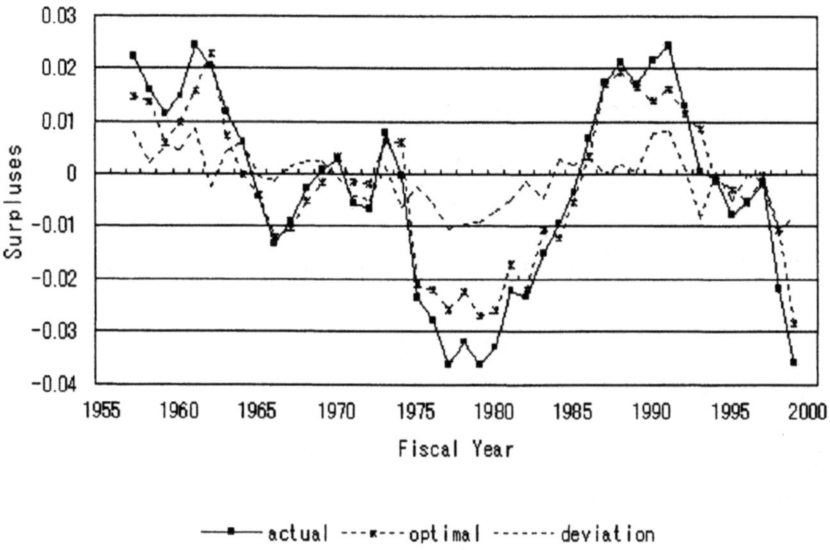

Figure1. Actual and optimal budget surpluses

4.4 Welfare loss

We define the social losses of taxation as

$$C = \sum_{t=1}^{T} (1+r)^{-t} \tau_t^2 Y_t \tag{29}$$

For analytical tractability, assuming that the growth rate of GDP is constant and equals the interest rate, (29) can be written as

$$C = \left(\sum_{t=1}^{T} \tau_t^2 \right) Y_1 \tag{30}$$

where Y_1 is the real GDP at the beginning of the sample period.

Similarly the social costs of taxation under the TSHcan be written as

$$C^* = \left(\sum_{t=1}^{T} \tau_t^{*2} \right) Y_1 \tag{31}$$

where τ^*_t is the optimal tax rate.

Using (30) and (31), we can obtain

$$C^*/C = \frac{(\sum_{t=1}^{T} \tau_t^{*2})}{(\sum_{t=1}^{T} \tau_t^2)} = \sum_{t=1}^{T} \left(\frac{\tau_t^2}{\sum_{t=1}^{T} \tau_t^2} \right) \left(\frac{\tau_t^{*2}}{\tau_t^2} \right) \tag{32}$$

The optimal budget surplus and the actual one can be written as

$$s^*_t = (1/\theta)t^*_t - g_t - ((1-\theta)/\theta)b_t \tag{33}$$

$$s_t = (1/\theta)t_t - g_t - ((1-\theta)/\theta)b_t \tag{34}$$

where t^* is the optimal tax revenue under the TSH

Using (33) and (34), we can obtain

$$\begin{aligned} \ln\left(\frac{\tau_t^{*2}}{\tau_t^2} \right) &= 2[\ln\tau_t^* - \ln\tau_t] \\ &= 2[(\ln\tau_t^* + \ln Y_t) - (\ln\tau_t + \ln Y_t)] \\ &= 2(t^* - t) \\ &= 2\theta(s_t^* - s_t) \end{aligned}$$

or

$$\left(\frac{\tau_t^{*2}}{\tau_t^2} \right) = \exp[2\theta(s_t^* - s_t)] \tag{35}$$

Substituting (35) into (32) yields

$$C^*/C = \sum_{t=1}^{T} \left(\frac{\tau_t^2}{\sum_{t=1}^{T} \tau_t^2} \right) \exp[2\theta(s_t^* - s_t)] \tag{36}$$

Therefore we can evaluate the welfare losses using (36).

The results are reported in Table 2. Over the entire sample period, the welfare loss, C/C^*, is slightly lower than one, although C/C^* should be more than one (because C^* is the welfare loss under the TSH). The reason why we underestimate the welfare loss is that the actual tax rates in the second half of the 1970s were lower than the optimal rate and thus the excess burdens of taxation were lower for that period. The low tax rates in the second half of the 1970s, however, led to an increase in public debts, which in turn would result in increase in tax rates in the future. Following the discussion above, we now calculate the welfare loss, assuming that an increase in government debts attributed to the deviations from the optimal path from 1974 to 1980 be reduced by an increase in tax revenues in the near future (from1996-2005). In this case, as shown in the middle panel of Table 2, the welfare loss is still small, although slightly higher than one.

It would be instructive to compare the welfare loss under the TSH with the one under some competing tax scheme. The lower panel of Table 2 reports the welfare loss, assuming that the government had followed a balanced budget policy over the entire sample period.[12] In this case the welfare loss is higher than the one under the scheme discussed above. Therefore we conclude that the fiscal policy implemented by Japanese government is not entirely consistent with the TSH, but that so far, the welfare loss due to deviations from the optimal path is not large.

Table 2. Welfare losses

variable	(1) Ω=0.95 ρ=0.95	(2) Ω=0.95 ρ=0.99	(3) Ω=0.99 ρ=0.95	(4) Ω=0.99 ρ=0.99
The entire sample period	0.995	0.995	0.994	0.994
The case in which tax rates are raised in the near futu re				
r=0.03	1.015	1.012	1.016	1.013
r=0.05	1.023	1.019	1.025	1.021
The case in which balanced budget policy had been implemented for the entire sample period	1.069	1.069	1.061	1.061

[12] Here we define a balanced budget policy as the case where s=0 for the entire sample period.

5. CONCLUSION

In this paper we have reviewed previous empirical studies on the TSH and tested its implication using postwar Japanese data. We have shown that the Japanese experience is not fully consistent with the hypothesis, but that so far, the welfare loss is not large.

A reason why the tax smoothing model is not successful in explaining the behavior of the budget deficits in Japan is that the government has not been a benevolent social planner that seeks an intertemporal optimization. As shown in Alesina and Tabellini (1990), when political power alternates randomly between competing political parties, the incumbent government will be tempted to leave a legacy of high debt for its successor, because the high debt can restrain the spending of the next government by commiting future tax revenues to debt services. This political game may lead to an accumulation of government debt beyond the optimal level prescribed by the tax smoothing model. In postwar Japan, the Liberal Democratic Party (LDP) has been in power as the predominant party for a long time, and thus it seems unlikely that the model developed by Alesina and Tabellini (1990) is valid in this circumstance. However, there is no denying that political conflicts may affect budgetary policy, as illustrated in the 1970s when opposition parties increased tin power and brought about the introduction of new social welfare programs. This issue remains unresolved

REFERENCES

Allesina, A. and G. Tabellini, 1990, A positive theory of fiscal deficits and government debt, *Review of Economic Studies* 57, 402 - 414.

Asako, K., T. Ito and K. Sakamoto, 1991,The rise and fall of deficit in Japan:1965-1990, *Journal of the Japanese and International Economies* 5, 451-472.

Barro, R., 1979, On the determination of the public debt, *Journal of Political Economy* 87, 940-971.

Barro, R., 1981, On the predictability of tax -rate changes, *NBER Working Paper* #636.

Campbell, J., 1987, Does saving anticipate declining labor income? An alternative test of the permanent income hypothesis, *Econometrica* 55, 1249-1273.

Campbell, J. and G. Mankiw, 1989, Consumption, income and interest rates: Reinterpreting the time series evidence, in Oliver Blanchard and Stanley Fischer eds. *NBER Macroeconomics Annual*, MIT Press.

Ghosh, A., 1995, Intertemporal tax-smoothing and the government budget surplus: Canada and the United States, *Journal of Money, Credit, and Banking* 27, 1033-1045.

Hall, R., 1978, Stochastic implications of the life cycle-permanent income hypothesis: Theory and evidence, *Journal of Political Economy* 86, 971-987.

Huang, Chao-Hsi and K. Lin, 1993, Deficits, government expenditures, and tax smoothing in the United States: 1929-1988, *Journal of Monetary Economics* 31, 317-339.

Mankiw, G., 1987, The optimal collection of seigniorage: Theory and evidence, *Journal of Monetary Economics* 20, 327-341.

Poterba, J. and J. Rotemberg, 1990, Inflation and taxation with optimizing governments,

Journal of Money, Credit, and Banking 22, 1-18.
Sahasakul, C., 1986, The U.S. Evidence on optimal taxation over time, *Journal of Monetary Economics* 18, 251-275.
Trehan, B. and C. Walsh, 1988, Common trends, the government's budget constraint, and revenue smoothing, *Journal of Economic Dynamics and Control* 12, 425-444.
Trehan, B. and C. Walsh, 1990, Seigniorage and tax smoothing in the United States: 1914-1986, *Journal of Monetary Economics* 25, 97-112.

Chapter 4

Sustainability Problem

Are Japanese Government Bonds sustainable?

1. LARGEST SUSTAINABLE DEBT

In the 1990s we have experienced a rapid increase in fiscal deficits. In the 1990s public spending and transfer payments have been gradually raised due to political pressure from interest groups, resulting in large budget deficits. The question of whether Japan's fiscal policy is sustainable, in the sense of being consistent with an intertemporal budget constraint, has long been a concern.

In order to explore theoretically the determinants of the largest amount of per capita debt that is consistent with competitive equilibrium b^*, consider a simple pure-exchange, two-period overlapping generations economy with constant population, which is consistent with the weak version of Ricardian debt neutrality. See Samuelson (1958) and Azariadis (1993).

The growth rate of population, *n*, is assumed to be zero. The per-capita saving function of the younger generations( ) is given by

$$s(r_{t+1}) = b_t \qquad (1)$$

where r is the interest rate and b is per capita debt. It is assumed that savings are increasing with the rate of interest. $\partial s/\partial r>0$. Then, from (1) we have

$$r_{t+1} = r(b_t) \qquad (1)'$$

The government budget constraint at time $t+1$ is given by

$$b_{t+1} = (1 + r_{t+1})b_t + g_{t+1} - \tau_{t+1} \tag{2}$$

where g is public spending and τ is tax revenues. The primary deficit q is defined as the difference between g and τ. Suppose for simplicity $q = 0$. Then, substituting (1)' into (2), we get

$$b_{t+1} = [1 + r(b_t)]b_t \tag{3}$$

Figure 1 describes equation (3) in the (b_{t+1}, b_t) plane. We call this curve Φ curve. Equation (3) has two stationary solutions. One of them is the origin, and the other equilibrium lies at the intersection of the 45 degree line with the phase line of equation (3), Φ curve. Figure 1 (i) is called the Samuelson case and Figure 1 (ii) is called the classical case.

Let us run a primary budget deficit $q_0 = b_0 > 0$ per capita at the beginning of time and preserve primary budget balance ($q_t = 0$) thereafter. How big can initial debt be? Figure 1 (i) shows that in the Samuelson case b_0 cannot exceed $s(n)$, the golden rule stock of per capita public debt, which is associated with point A. Figure 1 (ii) shows that in the classical case b_0 cannot exceed zero. Hence, the largest amount of per capita public debt that is consistent with competitive equilibrium b^* is either zero or $s(n)$, whichever is greater. $b^* = \max[0, s(n)]$. As shown in Azariadis (1993), when the primary deficit q increases, b^* will be reduced.

If $b_0 > s(n)$, the interest rate needed to induce households voluntary to hold b_0 would exceed the growth rate n in each period. National debt would grow faster than the economy, with debt service surpassing in finite time the maximal flow of saving which the household sector is capable of. The government debt will not be held by the household any more and the government goes bankrupt.

2. EXAMPLES

Identical households have the following utility function

$$u = c_1^t c_2^t$$

where c_1^t is the first-period consumption of generation t and c_2^t is the second period consumption of generation t. Endowment vector is (e_1, e_2), where the second-period endowment e_2 is smaller than the first-period endowment e_1.

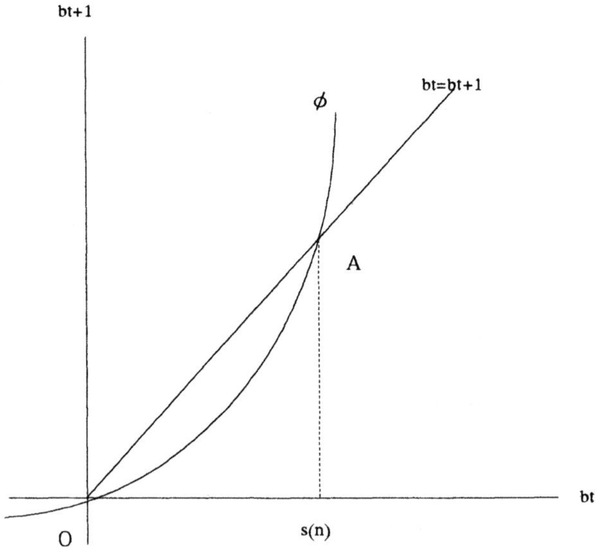

Figure 1(i). The Samuelson case

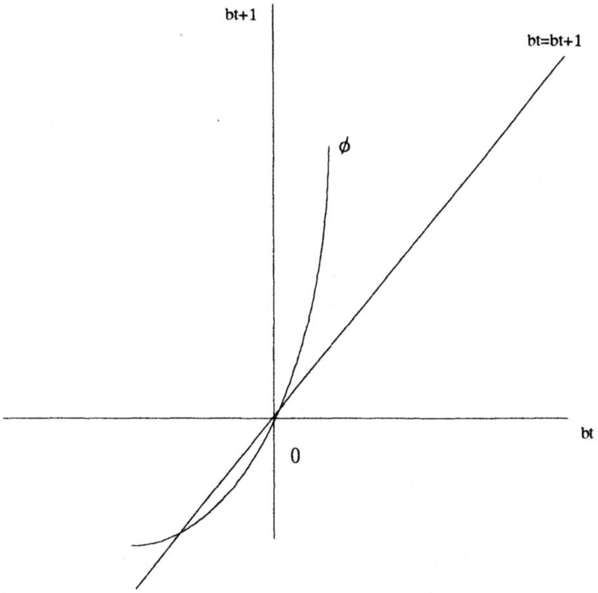

Figure 1(ii). The classical case

Fiscal policy is given by the set (g, τ_1, τ_2), where g is per capita government spending, τ_1 is lump sum taxes levied in the younger period, and τ_2 is lump sum taxes levied in the older period. Assuming for simplicity that the primary deficit q is zero, the government budget constraint is given by

$$\tau_1 + \tau_2 = g \tag{2)'}$$

Or

$$b_2 = (1+r_2)b_1 \tag{2)"}$$

It is assumed that $\tau_1 < e_1$, $g < e_2$; and beginning-of-time national debt b_0 is zero.

The lifetime budget constraint of the representative household is

$$c_1^t + \frac{c_2^t}{1+r_2} = e_1 - \tau_1 + \frac{e_2 - \tau_2}{1+r_2},$$

which implies a savings function of the form

$$s_1 = e_1 - \tau_1 - c_1^t = \frac{1}{2}[e_1 - \tau_1 + \frac{e_2 - \tau_2}{1+r_2}]$$

Considering (2)", the equilibrium sequence of national debt must then satisfy the equation

$$2b_1 = e_1 - \tau_1 - \frac{(e_2 - \tau_2)b_1}{b_2}$$

Stationary solutions are $b = 0$ at $1+r = (e_2 - \tau_2)/(e_1 - \tau_1)$ and $b = [e_1 - \tau_1 - (e_2 - \tau_2)]/2$ at $r = 0$. The latter is an asymptotically unstable equilibrium if $e_1 - \tau_1 > e_2 - \tau_2$.

The largest sustainable value of public debt b^* is hence given by

$$b^* = Max[0, \frac{e_1 - \tau_1 - (e_2 - \tau_2)}{2}] \tag{4}$$

Equation (4) implies that b^* is increasing with the first-period disposable income ($e_1 - \tau_1$) and is decreasing with the second-period disposable income ($e_2 - \tau_2$). An increase in τ_1 with a decrease in τ_2 means an intergenerational transfer from young to old. Thus, from (4) we can say that the higher the intergenerational transfer from young to old, the smaller the amount of b^*.

Given public consumption g per capita, the largest sustainable value of public debt per capita is attained if τ_1 is as small as possible, that is, at $\tau_1 = 0$, $\tau_2 = g$. Then, the largest amount of per capita deficit is

$$b^* = \frac{e_1 - e_2 + g}{2} \tag{4)'$$

which is positive when$e_1 + g > e_2$.

3. SUSTAINABILITY TESTS

As shown in sections 3.1 and 3.2, the higher the primary surplus, the propensity to save, the growth rate, or the intergenerational transfer from old to young, the more likely the sustainability problem will be alleviated. Put differently, either an increase in public spending or a decrease in tax revenues (an increase in transfer payments) contributes to an increase in the primary deficit, resulting in a higher pressure on the sustainabilityproblem.

As explained in chapter 1, fiscal deficits in the 1980s were reduced, mainly by cutting public spending to a great extent in the first half of the 1980s and by collecting taxes in the second half of the 1980s. In the 1990s we have experienced a rapid increase in fiscal deficits. In the 2000s it would be expected that an increase in transfer payments (a decrease in net tax revenues) due to aging would contribute to higher primary deficits. It is very important to restrain the increasing trend in transfer payments.

There have been a few analyses on the sustainability problem in the government debt in Japan. So long as we use the data until 1990, it seems that the government debt has been sustainable in Japan. However, as explained in section 1, fiscal deficits have increased rapidly since 1990. We are not sure if the present fiscal system in Japan is sustainable in the long run.

We survey the literature on sustainability of government bond before our test.

Hamilton and Flavin (1986) define the sustainability of government debt as follows. Government budget constraint in period t is expressed as

$$G_t + (1 + r_t)B_t = R_t + B_{t+1},$$

where G_t, R_t, r_t, and B_t denote aggregate real government expenditure (excluding interest payment), aggregate real tax revenue, real interest rate, and aggregate real bonds outstanding (at the beginning of period), respectively. We can rewrite as

$$B_{t+1} = E_t[\sum_{i=1}^{n}\{\prod_{j=1}^{i}(\frac{1}{1+r_{t+j}})\}(R_{t+i} - G_{t+i})] + E_t[\prod_{j=1}^{n}(\frac{1}{1+r_{t+j}})B_{t+n+1}]$$

where $Q_t \equiv R_t - G_t$.

Hamilton and Flavin (1986) define the government budget satisfies

$$\lim_{n\to\infty} E_t[\prod_{j=1}^{n}(\frac{1}{1+r_{t+j}})B_{t+n+1}] = 0 \qquad (5)$$

as the condition of sustainability of government bond. Equation (5) means no Ponzi game condition in dynamic macroeconomic models. Therefore we can confirm the sustainability of government bond by testing the following A is significantly equal to 0;

$$\lim_{n\to\infty} E_t[\prod_{j=1}^{n}(\frac{1}{1+r_{t+j}})B_{t+n+1}] = A \qquad A\text{: constant}$$

Hamilton and Flavin (1986), and Fukuda and Teruyama (1994) estimate the following regression to test the sustainability;

$$B_t = c_0 + A(1+r)^t + c_1 B_{t-1} + \cdots + c_p B_{t-p} + d_1 Q_{t-1} + d_2 Q_{t-2} + \cdots + d_p Q_{t-p} + u_t \qquad (6)$$

where u_t denotes a error term.

They assume that (expected) real interest rate is constant over time, and expectations and error terms of the regression satisfy the relation that the term of $E_t[\sum_{i=1}^{\infty}(\frac{1}{1+r})^i Q_{t+i}]$ depends on Q_{t-1}, Q_{t-2}, ..., Q_{t-p}, serial correlation of error terms is eliminated by using the variables, B_{t-1}, B_{t-2}, ..., B_{t-p}. If the estimator of A in equation (6) is significantly equal to 0, they conclude the government bondis sustainable.

In estimating equation (6), Hamilton and Flavin (1986) use the (expected) real interest rate that is assumed to be constant over time as the discount factor. However, it is not the best one as the discount factor, because the (expected) real interest rate varies with the business cycle and monetary policy. Wilcox (1989) tests the sustainability using a realized real interest rate (= nominal interest rate minus inflation rate) as the discount factor. Blanchard, Chouraqui, Hagemann, and Sartor (1990), and Uctum and Wickens (1997) rewrite equation (6) as per GDP term, which both sides in equation (6) are divided by GDP. Then they use realized real interest rate minus realized real growth rate as the discount factor. Moreover we have another sample of the discount factor.

Bohn (1995) builds a stochastic economy model with infinite horizon, and shows a condition on sustainability of government bond under dynamic efficiency. Instead of a real interest rate he uses the marginal rate of substitution between present and future consumption as the discount factor.

This economy consists of a representative household and the government. There are exogenous stochastic streams of real tax revenue, R_t, real government expenditure, G_t, and real income, Y_t.[1] The government issues bonds as a contingent security. The representative household earns his/her income, and decides real (private) consumption (C_t), and saving to maximize his/her intertemporal utility in each period. Under a certain assumption, intertemporal government budget constraint is expressed as

$$B_t = \sum_{i=0}^{n} E_t[\rho_{t,i}(R_{t+i} - G_{t+i})] + E_t[\rho_{t,n}B_{t+n}]$$

where $\rho_{t,i} \equiv \delta^i \dfrac{U'(C_{t+i})}{U'(C_t)}$ denotes marginal rate of substitution between consumptions in period t and t+1, $U(C_t)$ denotes instantaneous utility of the representative household, and $\delta>0$ denotes subject discount factor of the representative household. Bohn (1995) proves that the condition on sustainability of government bonds under the above economy is

$$\lim_{n\to\infty} E_t[\rho_{t,n}B_{t+n}] = 0 \qquad \forall t. \tag{5)'$$

Equation (5)' is a version of equation (5) in a stochastic economy.

We set an alternative hypothesis against the null hypothesis that the government bondsatisfy equation (5) as

$$\lim_{n\to\infty} E_t[\rho_{t,n}B_{t+n}] = A \neq 0.$$

Intertemporal government budget constraint ($n\to\infty$) is expressed as

$$E_t[B_t - A - \sum_{i=0}^{\infty} \rho_{t,i}Q_{t+i}] = 0.$$

[1] We assume that $G_t \le Y_t$. We also assume households are homogenous, but obtain the same result as Bohn(1995) that assumes households are heterogeneous.

To use GMM (generalized method of moment) developed by Hansen and Singleton (1982) we define the error termε_{t+1} as

$$\varepsilon_{t+1}(\theta) = B_t - A - \sum_{i=0}^{\infty} \rho_{t,i} Q_{t+i}$$

θ denotes a vector whose elements are estimators. From the above equations, we obtain

$$E_t[\varepsilon_{t+1}(\theta)] = 0.$$

Now we specify the instantaneous utility of the representative household (U) as follows.

$$U(C_t) = \frac{C_t^{1-\gamma} - 1}{1-\gamma} \qquad \gamma > 0$$

Then $\rho_{t,i} = \delta^i (\frac{C_{t+i}}{C_t})^{-\gamma}$. To test the sustainability, we have the following equation

$$E_t[B_t - A - \sum_{i=0}^{\infty} \delta^i (\frac{C_{t+i}}{C_t})^{-\gamma} Q_{t+i}] = 0.$$

Bohn (1998) proposed a new method different from existing tests for sustainability of government debt, which is based on estimating a transversality condition (5) and on cointegration methods.[2] His test has better properties than the conventional tests.

His test is the following. Fiscal policy satisfies the intertemporal budget constraint, i.e. the condition on sustainability of government debt, if the primary surplus to GDP (q_t) increases with the ratio of (start-of-period) debt to GDP (b_t) .[3] Suppose we express a relation between the two as

$$q_t = f(b_t) + \mu_t \tag{8}$$

[2] The tests of sustainability with cointegration methods are provided by Trehan and Walsh (1988), Hakkio and Rush (1991), Hang (1991), Ahemd and Rogers (1995), and so on.

[3] We define that $q_t \equiv (R_t - G_t)/ Y_t$, and $b_t \equiv B_t / Y_t$.

where other determinants, μ_t, is bounded and the present value of future GDP is finite. Then, government debt satisfies a transversality condition (5) if there is a debt-GDP ratio $\hat{b}$ such that $f'(b_t) \geq \beta > 0$ for all $b_t \geq \hat{b}$ (where β is a positive constant). Bohn found that an increase in the ratio of government debt to GDP raised the ratio of primary surplus to GDP for 1916-1995 in the U.S. It follows that U.S. fiscal policy satisfied an intertemporal budget constraint. Thus we can confirm that sustainability of government debt must satisfy the condition $f'(b_t) > 0$ (when the present value of future GDP is finite).[4]

Let us set $f(b_t) = \beta b_t$ as a special case of equation (8), that is,

$$q_t = \beta b_t + \alpha_0 + \alpha_G \mathrm{GVAR}_t + \alpha_Y \mathrm{YVAR}_t + \varepsilon_t, \tag{9}$$

where GVAR_t is a measure of temporary government expenditure, YVAR_t is a measure of cyclical variations in GDP. $\mathrm{GVAR}_t \equiv (G_t - G^*_t)/Y_t$, and $\mathrm{YVAR}_t \equiv (U_t - U^m)(G^*_t/Y_t)$, where G_t, G^*_t, U_t, and U^m denote real government expenditure, the permanent component of G_t, the unemployment rate and the median of U_t for the sample period, respectively.

We also assume $f(b_t) = \beta b_t + \gamma(b_t - \bar{b})^2$ instead of (8). Then, in place of (9) we have

$$q_t = \beta b_t + \gamma(b_t - \bar{b})^2 + \alpha_0 + \alpha_G \mathrm{GVAR}_t + \alpha_Y \mathrm{YVAR}_t + \varepsilon_t, \tag{10}$$

where $\bar{b}$ denotes the average of b_t for the sample period. We estimate both equations (9) and (10).

4. EVIDENCE IN JAPAN

We apply Bohn (1998)'s method to the test on the sustainability of Japanese government debt. We focus on the (national) General Account in Japan. We set the sample period as FY 1956-1998 and FY 1965-1998; FY 1965 is the year that Japanese government begun to issue debt in the General Account after WWII.

We make data on GVAR_t and YVAR_t in (9) or (10). Unfortunately, we cannot directly get data on G^*_t and U^m from official statistics. To make data on G^*_t in Japan, we use Beveridge and Nelson (1981) decomposition of real government expenditure into temporary and permanent components. For FY 1955-1998, the median of U_t, U^m, is equal to 0.021.

[4] Notice that this condition is a sufficient condition on sustainability of the government bond.

In estimating these equations, there exists serial correlation in the error terms of these equations. Hence we use the maximum likelihood estimation. Estimates of equation (9) are reported in regressions (I), (II), (V), and (VI) in Table 1. Also estimates of equation (10) are reported in regressions (III), (IV), (VII), and (VIII) in Table 1. Regressions (I)-(IV) show results for the sample period FY 1956-1998, and regressions (V)-(VIII) show results for the period FY 1965-1998. ρ in Table 1 denotes the estimator of first order autocorrelation of the error term.

Table1. Test for sustainability
Dependent variable: q_t
Maximum likelihood estimation with annual data

Sample	1956-1998				1965-1998			
	(I)	(II)	(III)	(IV)	(V)	(VI)	(VII)	(VIII)
Intercept	0.0039	0.0042	0.0034	0.0039	-0.0238	-0.0254	-0.0279	-0.0292
	(0.228)	(0.256)	(0.197)	(0.231)	(-2.025)	(-1.887)	(-2.140)	(-2.090)
b_t	0.0056	0.0037	-0.0020	-0.0036	0.0820	0.0815	0.0898	0.0847
	(0.110)	(0.075)	(-0.036)	(-0.067)	(2.019)	(1.787)	(2.247)	(1.886)
GVAR	-0.0231		-0.0288		0.6458		0.6499	
	(-0.226)		(-0.276)		(1.659)		(1.603)	
YVAR	-17.6178	-17.2851	-19.0126	-18.4708	-23.4328	-24.1307	-26.6392	-27.3682
	(-2.832)	(-2.893)	(-2.633)	(-2.688)	(-3.531)	(-3.570)	(-2.989)	(-3.182)
$(b_t - \bar{b})^2$			0.0544	0.0490			0.0587	0.0738
			(0.392)	(0.361)			(0.473)	(0.555)
ρ	0.9232	0.9223	0.9245	0.9234	0.7594	0.8302	0.7254	0.8155
	(17.927)	(17.964)	(18.057)	(18.054)	(7.003)	(9.435)	(6.148)	(8.725)
log L	149.232	149.204	149.319	149.276	119.178	117.915	119.279	118.078
adj. R^2	0.802	0.808	0.801	0.806	0.812	0.798	0.807	0.794
std. error	0.0082	0.0081	0.0082	0.0081	0.0076	0.0078	0.0078	0.0079
D.W.	1.457	1.466	1.478	1.487	1.808	1.686	1.816	1.706

Notes
1. The above parentheses indicate the t-values using White's consistent covariance.
2. D.W. denotes Durbin-Watson statistic.

For the sample period FY 1956-1998, estimators of β, coefficient of b, in the linear equation (9) are not significant. Also estimators of the first-order and second-order terms in the quadratic equation (10) are insignificant. We cannot find a positive response of the primary surplus-GDP ratio to changes in the debt-GDP ratio in the Japanese (national) General Account for FY 1956-1998.

For FY 1965-1998, the estimator β is significantly positive in regression (V). As the estimator of GVAR is not significant in this regression, we exclude GVAR and re-estimate the equation (9). Its result is reported in regression (VI). The estimator of β is insignificant in regression (VI). Similarly, estimators of the first-order and second-order terms are insignificant in regression (VIII). These results do not support the hypothesis that Japanese government debt satisfies a transversality condition for FY 1965-1998.

5. CONCLUSION

From the above analysis, we cannot reject the hypothesis that the Japanese national debt has not been sustainable at least in recent years. An intuitive explanation is as follows. We draw a scatter plot of the primary surplus-GDP ratio against the debt-GDP ratio in Figure 2. Until early 1990s, Japanese fiscal policy held the quadratic relation between the two. Recently, Japanese fiscal policy deviates from the relation excessively. This is one of the reasons we obtain the above result in this section. Hence, it is important to reduce the government deficitin the near future.

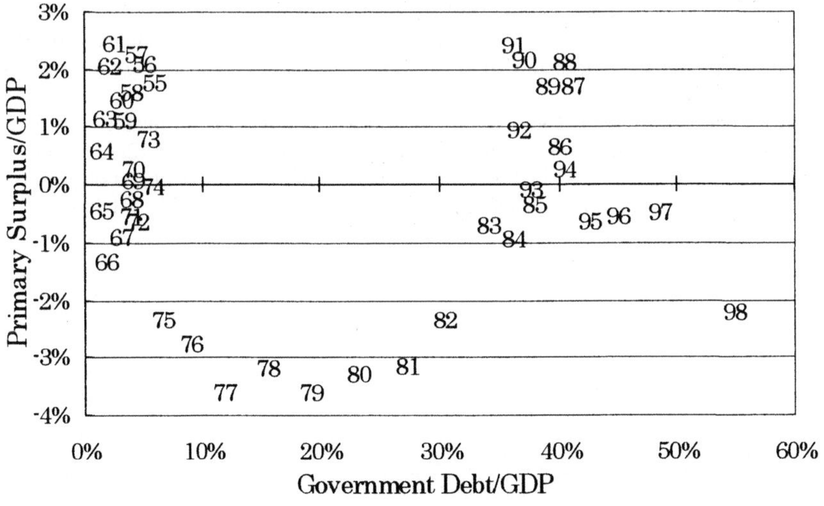

Figure 2. Primary surplus and government debt 1955-1998

REFERENCES

Ahemd, S., and J. Rogers, 1995, Government budget deficits and trade deficits: Are present value constraints satisfied in long-run data?, *Journal of Monetary Economics* 36, 351-374.

Azariadis, C., 1993, *Intertemporal Macroeconomics*, Blackwell.

Beveridge, S. and C.R. Nelson, 1981, A new approach to decomposition of economic time series into permanent and transitory components with particular attention to measurement of the 'business cycle,' *Journal of Monetary Economics* 7, 151-174.

Blanchard, O., J.-C. Chouraqui, R.P. Hagemann and N. Sartor, 1990, The sustainability of fiscal policy: New answers and to an old question, *OECD Economic Studies* 15, 7-36.

Bohn, H., 1995, The sustainability of budget deficits in a stochastic economy, *Journal of Money, Credit, and Banking* 27, 257-271.

Bohn, H., 1998, The behavior of U.S. public debt and deficits, *Quarterly Journal of Economics* 113, 949-963.

Diamond, P. A., 1965, National debt in a neoclassical growth model, *American Economic Review* 55, 1126-1150.

Fukuda, S. and H. Teruyama, 1994, The sustainability of budget deficits in Japan, *Hitotsubashi Journal of Economics* 35, 109-119.

Hakkio, C.S. and M. Rush, 1991, Is the budget deficits "too large?," *Economic Inquiry* 29, 429-445.

Hamilton, J.D. and M.A. Flavin, 1986, On the limitations of government borrowing: A framework for empirical testing, *American Economic Review* 76, 808-816.

Hang, A.A., 1991, Cointegration and government borrowing constraints: Evidence for the United States, *Journal of Business and Economic Statist ics* 9, 97-101.

Hansen, L.P. and K.J. Singleton, 1982, Generalized instrumental variables estimation of nonlinear rational expectations models, *Econometrica* 50, 1269-1286.

Samuelson, P., 1958, An exact consumption-loan model of interest with or without thesocial contrivance of money, *Journal of Political Economy* 66, 467-482.

Uctum, M. and M. Wickens, 1997, Debt and deficit ceilings, and sustainability of fiscal policies: An international analysis, *Centre for Economic Policy Research Discussion Paper* # 1612.

Trehan, B. and C.E. Walsh, 1988, Common trends, the government budget constraint, and revenue smoothing, *Journal of Economic Dynamics and Control* 12, 425-444.

Wilcox, D.W., 1989, The sustainability of government deficits: Implications of presentvalue borrowing constraint, *Journal of Money, Credit, and Banking* 21, 291-306.

Chapter 5

Government Deficits in an Aging Japan

1. INTRODUCTION

This chapter examines the effects of government deficits and public pension policies on the tax burden, capital accumulation and economic welfare in the transition to an aging Japan by applying a simulated method in the expanded life cyclegeneral equilibriumgrowth model.

In the literature of government debt policies of Japan, the effects of government deficit policies have been discussed in different ways. Asako et al (1993) did empirical research on government deficitspolicies of Japan and Doi and Nakazato (1998) empirically discussed the sustainability of government deficits policies. Kawagoe (2000) recently presented several proposals by simulating the effect of government deficitspolicies of Japan based on OECD figures.

The effects of an aging population, and/or the effects of several tax policies and public pension policies in the transition to an aging Japan have also been discussed by applying the simulated overlapping generations models in the literature. A simulated Overlapping Generations Model originated by Auerbach and Kotlikoff (1983 and 1987) was first applied to the analysis of the effect of tax policies and the public pension policies of Japan by Homma et al (1987), and the existing studies have expanded the Auerbach/Kotlikoff model to discuss several government policies in the transition to an aging Japan (Iwamoto (1990), Iwamoto et al (1991 and 1993), Atoda and Kato (1993), and Kato (1998)). Hatta and Oguchi (1999) recently emphasised the intergenerational redistribution of income through the existing pay-as-you-go public pension scheme in Japan by applying their own simulated method.

Although these two literatures have been well developed, both government deficit policies and public pension policies have not been discussed comprehensively. Most of baby boomers in Japan have yet reached the age of pension beneficiaries; current pay-as-you-go type pension fund has more contributors than beneficiaries. Thus, the public pension fund earns a certain amount of surpluses so far. The effect of outstanding government deficits should be comprehensively discussed in relation to the existing public pension fund, since outstanding government debts and the public pension fund affect capital accumulation oppositely. Aso (1997 and 1998) mentioned the effect of outstanding government deficits in the transition to an aging Japan, but his main concern was to discuss the effect of an aging population on the public pension scheme. Thus, the main aim of this chapter is to comprehensively discuss the effect of outstanding government deficits in the transition to an aging Japan by proposing several government deficit policies, as well as the public pension scheme, within the simulated overlapping generations framework

Although the model constructed in this chapter mainly depends on Kato (1998), the following two aspects are expanded[1]: One aspect is that in the simulation analysis of this paper the latest version of the actual forecasted population data estimated in 1997 by the National Institute of Population and Social Security Research have been used, since nothing is more natural in a simulation analysis than using data which are as realistic as possible. The other aspect is the explicit incorporation of government deficits into the model. Since the main concern of Kato (1998) was to discuss the effect of the transition of an aging population in Japan through the existing public pension scheme, little attention was paid to the effect of outstanding government debts in Japan. In this chapter, as much real Japanese government deficit data is used as possible, and several scenarios regarding the future path of outstanding government debtswill be considered.

This chapter is organised as follows: Section 2 describes the basic model employed in the simulation analysis and Section 3 shows the method of the simulation analysis and its assumptions. Section 4 evaluates several scenarios of future government deficit policies by comparing the effects on macroeconomic variables as well as welfare of different generations. Section 5 summarises and concludes this chapter.

[1] See also Kato (2001), where productive public capital was also incorporated.

2. THE MODEL

In an economy, where each year is assumed to be a discrete time-unit, there are three types of agents, households, firms, and a government. The behaviour of each agent is described as follows:

Households:

Each generation is assumed to have the same income, mortality rate, and utility function. It is also assumed that each generation appears in the economy as a decision-making unit at the age of 21 and live to a maximum of 100 with a certain probability of death for every period. When $q_{j+1,j}$ is the conditional probability that a household of age j+20 survives to age j+21, the probability of a household of age 21 surviving until s+21 can be expressed as

$$S_S = \prod_{j=1}^{S-1} q_{j+1,j},$$

where $q_{j+1,j}$ is calculated from the actual data estimated by the National Institute of Population and Social Security Research in 1997. Assuming that each household makes lifetime decisions about the allocation of wealth between consumption and savings in order to maximise its expected utility, the expected utility at age s+20 would be

$$U = \sum_{s=1}^{80} S_s (1+\delta)^{-(s-1)} \frac{C_s^{1-\frac{1}{\gamma}}}{1-\frac{1}{\gamma}}, \tag{1}$$

where C_s represents consumption at age s+20, δ the discount rate, and γ the elasticity of intertemporal substitution.

It is assumed that each household at age s+20 has the budget constraint such that

$$\begin{aligned} A_{s+1} &= [1+(1-\tau_r(t))r(t)]A_s + (1-\tau(t)-\tau_p(t))w(t)e_s \\ &\quad + b_s + a_s - (1+\tau_c(t))C_s, \end{aligned} \tag{2}$$

where A_s represents the amount of assets held by each household at the beginning of age s+20, $r(t)$ is the interest rate at period t, e_s is the efficiency unit of labour which depends on age, and w is the wage rate per efficiency unit of labour. For the sake of brevity, the labour supply is assumed to be inelastic and the labour supply after retirement is assumed to be zero.[2] All tax systems are based on proportional taxation, with τ_y representing the wage income tax rate, τ_r the interest income tax rate, τ_c the consumption tax rate, and τ_p the contribution to the public pension scheme. In order to reflect the actual aspect of the existing public pension scheme in Japan, 1/3 of the total amount of the public pension benefits is assumed to be financed by taxes. b_s is the expected amount of post-taxed bequests to be inherited.[3] For simplicity, bequests are assumed to be inherited at age 50.[4] b_s is the amount of public pension benefits, which is assumed such that

$$\begin{cases} b_s = \beta H & (s \geq RP) \\ b_s = 0 & (s < RP), \end{cases}$$

$$H = \frac{1}{IR} \sum_{s=1}^{IR} w(t) e_s ,$$

where β and H denote the replacement ratio and the average annual remuneration, respectively. RP+20 and IR+20 denote the age at which households start to receive public pension benefits and the retirement age respectively.[5]

Furthermore, the following two constraints are incorporated in addition to the conventional budget constraint. The first constraint is on the consumption level such that

$$C_s \geq C_{MIN} , \tag{3}$$

[2] For the estimation of the efficiency unit of labour e_s, the following equation has been estimated:

$$e = a_0 + a_1 A + a_2 A^2 + a_3 L + a_4 L^2 ,$$

where A represents age, L the length of employment, and e the wage rate per hour, respectively. The above equation has been estimated under the assumption that workers do not change their jobs during their working periods, thus implying that it might have an upward bias. However, the author does not believe that this bias would be crucial for the aim of this chapter. By using the data from "The Investigation of the Wage Structure (Chingin Kozo Kiso Chosa) in 1994," the above variables have been estimated as

a_0	a_1	a_2	a_3	a_4
-0.1537	0.05539	-0.0007595	0.1045	-0.001901
(-0.5363)	(2.865)	(-4.019)	(4.823)	(-3.243)

[3] It is assumed that there is no private pension market.

[4] Several patterns of the timing when bequests are inherited have been examined in Atoda and Kato (1993).

[5] Since the actual public pension system in Japan is a double indexation system, the above assumptions would not reflect reality. This drawback should be improved.

where C_{MIN} denotes the minimum consumption level. The other constraint is the households' liquidity constraint. Considering the uncertainty of actual lifetime in the model, the households are apt to see their public pension benefits, which they will receive from the age 65, as security and produce a high level of consumption when they are young, since the weight placed on consumption at old age is extremely small due to their uncertainty of their lifetimes, resulting in a very small amount of consumption when they are old. However, in reality the public pension benefits cannot actually offer security. Given that the assets at the end of each previous period are negative, a liquidity constraint is imposed on consumption at the present period in this way:

$$C_s \le [1+(1-\tau_r)r(t)]A_s + (1-\tau_y(t)-\tau_p(t))w(t)e_s \\ + b_s + a_s \equiv DY_s. \tag{4}$$

Now, suppose that each household maximises its utility under these constraints, and the maximisation of (1) subject to (2), (3), and (4) yields (see Appendix 1 for the detailed deduction)

$$C_s = \{ANC_s C_1^{-1/\gamma} + AOB_s\}^{-\gamma}, \tag{5}$$

where[6]

$$ANB(t) = \frac{PC(t)}{PC(1)\prod_{t=1}^{80} ARA(t)}$$

$$ANC_s = \frac{ANB(t) S_1 (1+\delta)^{(s-1)}}{S_s},$$

$$PC(t) = 1 + \tau_c(t),$$

$$ARA(t) = 1 + (1-\tau_r(t))r(t),$$

and

$$AOB_s = \frac{(1+\delta)^{(s-1)}}{S_s} \times$$

$$\left\{ ANB(t)\left[\phi_{11} - \phi_{21} - PC(1)\sum_{s=2}^{80} \phi_{2s} DY_s \left(\prod_{t=1}^{s-1} ARA(t) \right)\right] + \phi_{2s} - \phi_{1s} \right\}$$

[6] $PC(1)$ expresses $PC(t)$ of households at age 21.

From (5), the optimal consumption behaviour of all ages can be derived, if the initial consumption level, C_1, is specified. And the savings level can be calculated from (2) and (5).

Firms:

Firms are assumed to have the followingCES production function:[7]

$$Y(t) = \psi\left[\varepsilon K(t)^{1-1/\sigma} + (1-\varepsilon)L(t)^{1-1/\sigma}\right]^{-(1-1/\sigma)}, \tag{6}$$

where $K(t)$ represents the total capital, $L(t)$ the labour supply measured by the efficiency unit, σ the parameter of the elasticity of substitution between $K(t)$ and $L(t)$, ε the weight parameter, and ψ the scale parameter. From the profit maximization of firms subject to (8), the first-order condition is derived to be:

$$\frac{w(t)}{r(t)} = \frac{1-\varepsilon}{\varepsilon}\left(\frac{K(t)}{L(t)}\right)^{1/\sigma}.$$

The property of a constant-return-to-scale production functionalso yields

$$Y(t) = w(t)L(t) + r(t)K(t).$$

Government:

Suppose that the government consists of a narrower government sector and a public pension sector. A narrower government sector is assumed to spend revenue on general government expenditure,[8] and 1/3 of the total amount of public pension benefits is assumed to be transferred from the account of the narrower government sector to the account of the public pension sector. The budget of the narrower government sector is assumed to be financed by collecting taxes as well as issuing government bonds The budget constraint on the narrower government sector at time$t$ is given by:

$$D(t+1) - D(t) = R(t) - G(t) - r(t)D(t) - Pen(t),$$

where $D(t)$, $R(t)$, and $G(t)$ denote the amount of outstanding government debts, total tax revenue and general government expenditure at time t, respectively. $Pen(t)$ is the amount of the transfer from the narrower

[7] The difference between age, generation and period must be distinguished. Denoting the generation I, the age s, and the period t, they are related to each other as follows: $t=I+s-1$.

[8] The narrower government sector consists of central as well as local government expenditure, transfers and the expenditure on public investment.

government sector to the public pension sector. The budget constraint on the public pension sector is given by:

$$F(t+1) - F(t) = r(t)F(t) + Pen(t) + P(t) - B(t),$$

where $F(t)$, $P(t)$ and $B(t)$ denote the amount of public pension fund, total public pension benefits, and the total amount of the contribution to a public pension scheme, respectively. $R(t)$, $P(t)$ and $B(t)$ are given by

$$R(t) = \tau_y(t)w(t)L(t) + \tau_r(t)r(t)AS(t) + \tau_c(t)AC(t) + \tau_h(t)BQ(t)$$

$$P(t) = \tau_p(t)w(t)L(t),$$

$$B(t) = \sum_{s=45}^{80} S_s N_s b_s,$$

where τ_h and N_s denote the inheritance tax rate and the sum of s-year-old generations at time t, respectively. $AS(t)$, $AC(t)$ and $BQ(t)$ denote the total amount of savings, consumption and bequests inherited by the generation of age 50 in the economy at time t, respectively, and given by

$$AS(t) = \sum_{s=1}^{80} S_s N_s A_s$$

$$AC(t) = \sum_{s=1}^{80} S_s N_s C_s$$

$$BQ(t) = \sum_{s=1}^{80} (1 - S_s) N_s A_s.$$

Market Equilibrium:

An equilibrium condition in the capital market is given by

$$AS(t) + F(t) = K(t) + D(t)$$

and in the goods market it is

$$Y(t) = AC(t) + (K(t+1) - K(t)) + G(t).$$

3. SIMULATION ANALYSIS

3.1 Structure and data

This section explores the effects of government deficits in transition to an aging Japan by applying the simulated method based on the model constructed in Section 2. In order to examine the effects of changes in the demographic structure caused by the transition to an aging population, especially when applying the simulated method, it is most natural to use population data which are as realistic as possible. Using the actual population data estimated in 1997 by the National Institute of Population and Social Security Research, this chapter has succeeded in reproducing these data exactly by applying the model constructed in Section 2. The demographic structure in this model has been generated by the following procedure.

<Population Structure>

All generations born before the generation of age 100 in 1990 (the generation born in 1890) are assumed to have the same birth and mortality rates as the generation of age 100 in 1990, so that the demographic structure of all generations born before 1890 is identical. It is also assumed that the population distribution will continue to be the same for each period from year 2100. Based on these assumptions, the actual population data estimated in 1997 by the Institute of Population and Social Security Research have been used for the periods from year 1996 to 2100 and the actual population data in "Population Census of Japan (Kokusei-chosa)" for the periods before 1996.[9] Such assumptions for the demographic structure were made because the latest actual data available were those of 1995 and the estimation made in 1997 by the Institute of Population and Social Security Research only covers the periods from 1995 to 2100.

All parameters in this chapter have been set so that the economic varia bles obtained from the actual Japanese data of 1997, such as the ratios of certain tax revenues to the total tax revenues, could be reproduced as precisely as possible. In other words, the induced estimation data of 1997 from the

[9] For the period prior to 1996, whenever the actual data from the Population Census of Japan (Kokusei-chosa), which is held only one every five years, was not available, actual population data from the "Simple Static Life Table" (from the Japanese Ministry of Health and Welfare) were used. The estimated number of people at the age of 100 for the periods from 1996 to 2100 has been calculated by using the data on survival probabilities based on sex and age from the estimation made in 1997 by the Institute of Population and Social Security Research. In the demographic structure the population distribution continues to be the same for each period prior to 1947, since it has not been possible to obtain this data from the Population Census of Japan.

simulation analysis has been set as close as possible to the real Japanese data of 1997.

<Outstanding Government debtsand Social Security Fund>

Until 1997 the actual data of outstanding government debts as well as of social security funds have been used. Outstanding government debts consist of central government debts and local governments debts.[10] The actual GDP data has also been used until 1997, and the bond-GDP ratio and the social security fund-GDP ratio prior to 1997 are both actual ratios in this chapter.

All parameters have been set so that the calculated values from the model could be reproduced as exactly as possible as shown in the following table 1.[11]

Table1. Values of 1997 (%)

	Actual values	Calculated values
Ratio of public to national income	37.78	36.52
Tax burden ratio	23.80	23.12
Social security contribution ratio	13.97	13.39
Contribution rate	18.0	18.7

$\alpha = 0.25, \gamma = 0.45, \delta = -0.035, \psi = 1.2, \varepsilon = 0.63, \sigma = 0.45$

3.2 Specification of parameters

The actual data of the bond-GDP ratio as well as of the social security fund-GDP ratio has been used in all periods until 1997 in this chapter. The actual data of the ratio of general government expenditure to GDP has also been used until 1997. The actual data of general government expenditure consists of central and local government consumption, public investment and

[10] The actual data of outstanding central government debts has been obtained from Budget Statistics (Zaisei Tokei) and that of outstanding local government debts from Annual Report on Local Governments Bonds (Chihosai Tokei Nenpo).

[11] According to the translation by Economic and Social Research Institute, Kokumin Hutanritsu, Sozei Hutanritsu, and Shakaihosyo Hutanritsu are translated into the ratio of public to national income, the tax burden ratio, and the social security contribution ratio in this chapter, respectively.

transfers.[12] The future values of general government expenditure have been given in this chapter under the assumption that they grow at the same rate as the rate of population aging

In this chapter the following four scenarios regarding future government deficits have been considered:[13] the ratio of outstanding government debts to GDP (the D-G ratio) has been assumed to converge to a 90% level in Case 1, a 40% level in Case 2, a 5% level in Case 3, and a 110% level in a steady state, respectively (see Figure 1). In Case 1 the amount of newly issued government bonds is assumed to decrease until the amount becomes zero, thus resulting in a higher steady state level of the D-G ratio than the actual level of the D-G ratio in 1997. In Case 2 a steady state level of the D-G ratio is assumed to converge to about a half of the actual level in 1997. In Case 3 government deficits are assumed to be nearly zero in a steady state. Case 4 corresponds to a proposal presented by Kawagoe (2000). Narrowed or widened government deficits are always followed by an increase or a decrease in tax rates. Thus, when the effects of future government deficit policies are explored, taxes associated with future government deficit policies must be specified. In this chapter a wage tax (-W) and a consumption tax (-C) have been used in each case, thus eight cases have been studied depending on the difference in taxation as follows (see Figure 1):

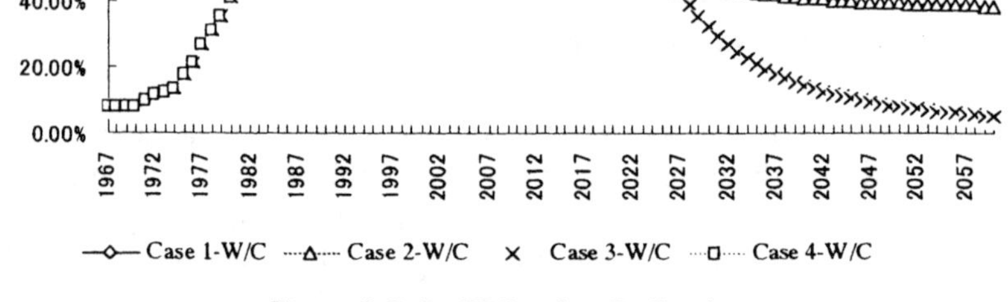

Figure 1. Debt-GDP ratios (D-G ratios)

[12] The transfer to a public pension sector is not included in this category.

[13] Since the purpose of this chapter is to investigate the effects of future government deficits, it is assumed that the future ratio of social security fund to GDP converges to the same value in all cases in a steady state under the assumption that the growth rate of the future ratio decreases through time until the growth rate becomes zero. The shortage of money spent in a public pension sector in each scenario is assumed to be financed all by an increase in the contribution rate.

<Case 1-W: 90% D-G Ratio>

The amount of newly issued government bonds is assumed to decrease until the amount becomes zero, thus resulting in a higher steady state level of the D-G ratio than the actual level of the D-G ratio in 1997. The ratio of outstanding government debts to GDP (the D-G ratio) converges to a 90 % level in a steady state. The shortage of money spent in a narrower government sector is assumed to be financed by a wage tax.

<Case 1-C: 90% D-G Ratio>

Apart from the way to finance the shortage of money spent in a narrower government sector, the future scenario is the same as that in Case 1-W. In this case, the shortage is assumed to be financed by a consumption tax

<Case 2-W: 40% D-G Ratio>

A steady state level of the D-G ratio is assumed to converge to a 40% level, about a half of the actual level in 1997. The shortage of money spent in a narrower government sector is assumed to be financed by a wage tax.

<Case 2-C: 40% D-G Ratio>

Apart from the way to finance the shortage of money spent in a narrower government sector, the future scenario is the same as that in Case 2-W. In this case, the shortage is assumed to be financed by a consumption tax

<Case 3-W: 5% D-G Ratio>

The government deficits are assumed to be nearly zero in a steady state. The shortage of money spent in a narrower government sector is assumed to be financed by a wage tax.

<Case 3-C: 5% D-G Ratio>

Apart from the way to finance the shortage of money spent in a narrower government sector, the future scenario is the same as that in Case 3-W. In this case, the shortage is assumed to be financed by a consumption tax

<Case 4-W: 110% D-G Ratio>

A steady state level of the D-G ratio is assumed to converge to a 110% level. This scenario corresponds to a proposal presented by Kawagoe (2000). The shortage of money spent in a narrower government sector is assumed to be financed by a wage tax.

<Case 4-C: 110% D-G Ratio>

Apart from the way to finance the shortage of money spent in a narrower government sector, the future scenario is the same as that in Case 4-W. In this case, the shortage is assumed to be financed by a consumption tax

4. THE RESULTS IN THE SIMULATION ANALYSIS

4.1 The effects on the ratio of public to national income

Figure 2 shows the future ratio of public to national income (Kokumin Hutanritsu: the P-N ratios) in each case. Figures 2-1 and 2-2 show the future ratio when the shortage of money is financed by a wage tax and a consumption tax respectively.

It is shown in Figure 2-1 that the ratio of public to national income (the P-N ratios) in Case 2 and 3 will increase after year 2010 compared to Case 1 and 4. The P-N ratio will increase up to 46.71% in year 2071 in Case 3, where the D-G ratio is assumed to continue to decrease even after year 2020. This is because a large increase in the wage tax rate is followed by a rapid increase in redeeming outstanding government deficitsat a relatively earlier stage in Case 3. On the other hand, the amount of outstanding government deficits will decrease in the future in Case 2 and 3 due to redeeming the deficits at a relatively earlier stage, and the P-N ratio in a steady state in Case 2 and 3 will converge to a relatively lower level compared to a level in Case 1 or 4, since a successive increase in the wage tax rate will be followed to finance interest payment incurred from the relatively higher amount of outstanding government deficits in Case 1 and 4 compared to Case 2 and 3. In Case 4, where the D-G ratio is assumed to converge to a 110% level in a steady state, the P-N ratio will increase up to 50.00% in year 2044. In Case 1 and 4, the D-G ratio will be maintained at high levels through time in the future, and the high P-N ratio will also continue through time in the future. Thus, the timing at the peak of the P-N ratio depends on the time when the government starts to redeem outstanding government deficits in the future, and a steady state level of the P-N ratio depends on the pattern of future government deficits

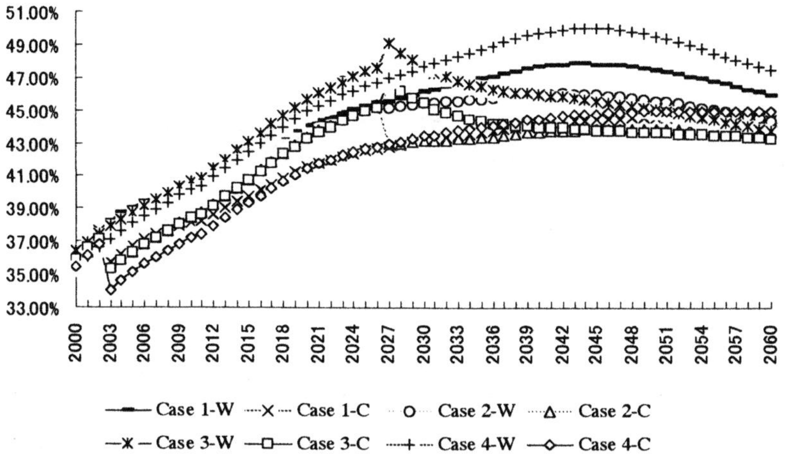

Figure 2.

Ratios of public to national income (P-N ratios, kokumin hutanritsu)

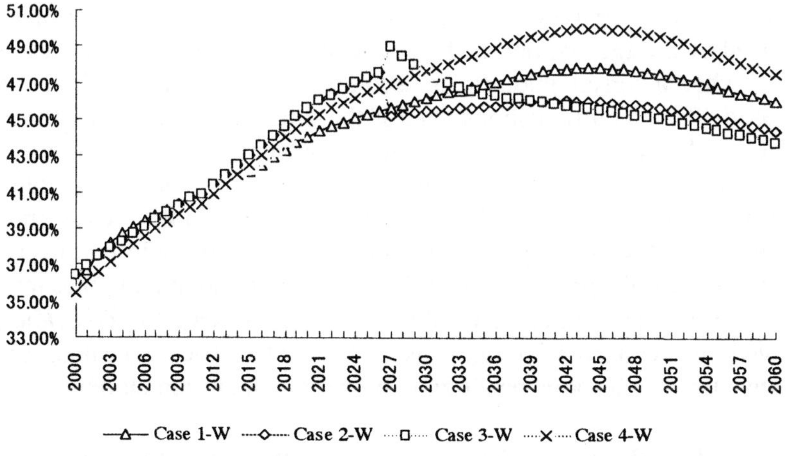

Figure2.1.

Ratios of public to national income (P-N ratios, kokumin futanritsu) , with a wage tax

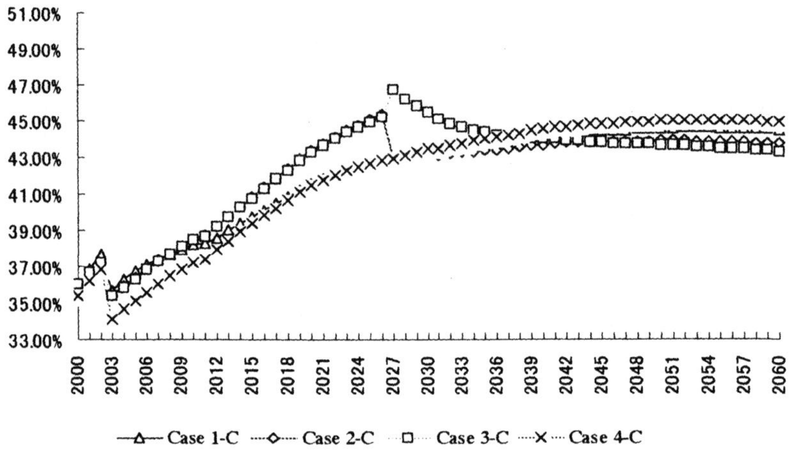

Figure 2.2.

Ratios of public to national income (P-N ratios, kokumin hutanritsu) , with a consumption tax

Figure 2-2 shows the future P-N ratio under four scenarios when the shortage of money spent in a narrower government sector is financed by a consumption tax. The trend through time is similar to that when the shortage is financed by a wage tax, but the level in each case is different: the levels in all cases when a consumption tax is used are lower than those when a wage tax is used. This is more distinguished if the difference is compared in Case 3 and Case 4. Even when the shortage is financed by consumption tax, a steady state level of the P-N ratio in Case 4 (-C) will be the highest. However, compared to Case 3 (-W), where the D-G ratio is assumed to converge to the lowest level, the P-N ratio in Case 4 (-C) will be lower than those in Case 3 (-W) prior to year 2055. Thus, even though a higher level of the D-G ratio is maintained, it would be possible to keep the P-N ratio at a lower level if a consumption tax is used. This is because a consumption tax will stimulate savings, thus resulting in higher capital accumulation.

4.2 The effects on the social security contribution ratio

The ratio of public to national income consists of the social security contribution ratio and the tax burden ratio. Figure 3 shows the future social security contribution ratio. As shown in Figure 3, the social security contribution ratio in all cases when a consumption tax is used is lower than that when a wage tax is used due to a positive effect of a consumption tax on capital accumulation.

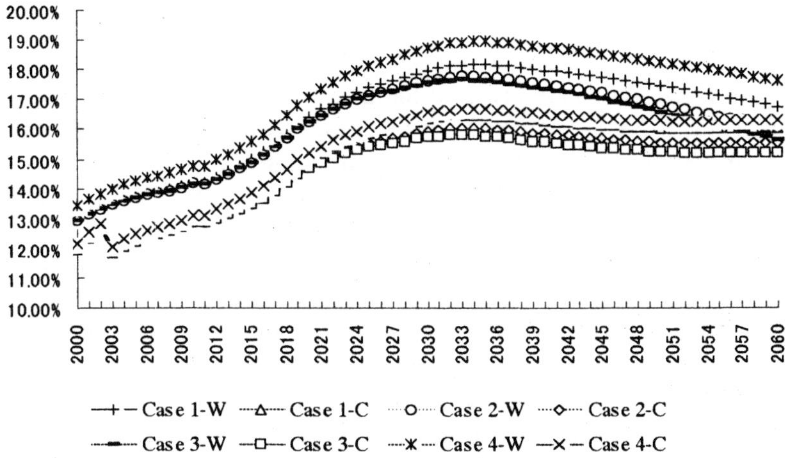

Figure 3. Social security contribution ratios (Shakai hosho hutanritsu)

Furthermore, an increase in the P-N ratio in trend can be explained by an increase in the social security contribution ratio by comparing Figure 3 with Figure 2. Especially after 2045, a decrease in the P-N ratio can be explained by the change in the social security contribution ratio

4.3 The Effects on utility

All of the cases have been evaluated by comparing their respective levels of utility. Setting different generations as I and the index measuring the utility level as EV, the definition of the utility level index of each generation is given by

$$EV(I) = \mu(p^0; p^1, y^1) / \mu(p^0; p^0, y^0),$$

where $\mu(\cdot)$ represents the money metric indirect utility function which is defined as

$$\mu(p^0; p^1, y^1) \equiv e(p^0, v(p^1, y^1)),$$

where $e(\ )$ and $v(\ )$ denote the expenditure function and the indirect utility function, respectively. $\boldsymbol{p}$ and y denote price vector and income, respectively, and the superscripts 0 and 1 imply the circumstances under a benchmark policy and those under each proposed policy, respectively. A generation born in 1990 is assumed to be a benchmark generation in this chapter, and the comparison in utility has been conducted under the assumption that p^0 and y^0 are the price vector and the income of a generation born in 1990 in Case 1-W. The price vector, p^0, consists of the interest rate, the wage rate, and the tax rates, which are given to the generation born in 1990 through its lifetime. Thus, if $EV(I)$ is greater (smaller) than 1, it implies that a proposed policy is preferable (not preferable) by generation I to a benchmark policy. Note that a benchmark policy is to maintain a 90 % le vel of the D-G ratio in a steady sate with a wage tax. Note also that $EV(I)$ measures the evaluation of different policies by each generation, but not the evaluation of a policy by different generations.[14]

Figure 4-1 emphasises the difference in the future utility levels when a wage tax is used. When the shortage of money spent in a narrower government sector is financed by a wage tax, the scenario that the D-G ratio converges to a 110% level in a steady state (Case 4-W) is not preferred by all future generations. The generations born after year 2026 prefer a 40% level of the D-G ratio (Case 2-W) to a 90% level of the D-G ratio (Case 1-W). The generations born after year 2035 prefer a zero level of the D-G ratio (Case 3-W) to a 90% level of the D-G ratio (Case 1-W). Furthermore, the generations born after year 2040 prefer a zero level of the D-G ratio (Case 3-W) to a 40% level of the D-G ratio (Case 2-W). This is because the per capita income level in Case 3-W is higher than that in Case 2-W among future generations, and this difference in income increases as more future generations are considered.

Figure 4-2 shows the future utility levels when a consumption tax is used. Figure 4-2 is depicted under the assumption that a benchmark case is Case 1-C in order to emphasise the difference in utility under proposed policies. In the case when the shortage of money is financed by a consumption tax, there are generations that prefer the scenario that the D-G ratio converges to a 110% level (Case 4-C) to the scenario that the D-G ratio converges to a 90% level (Case 1-C). The generations born prior to late 2020 prefer the scenario with a 110% steady state D-G ratio to the scenario with a 90% steady state level. This result can be interpreted as follows: In Case 4, the generations born in earlier periods would obtain more benefits since a relatively bw tax (wage or consumption tax) is imposed in earlier periods and a successively high tax is imposed in future periods due to interest payment incurred from the higher amount of outstanding government deficits in the future. In Case 4-C, where a consumption tax is used, there is a positive effect of consumption taxation to stimulate savings, thus resulting in higher income.

[14] Suppose that in Case 2-W $EV_{2\text{-}W}(I_1)$=1.1, $EV_{2\text{-}W}(I_2)$=1.3, and in Case 3-C $EV_{3\text{-}C}(I_1)$=1.2, $EV_{3\text{-}C}(I_2)$=1.5, are given to generation I_1 and I_2, respectively. This implies that both generation I_1 and I_2 prefer Case 2-W and Case 3-C to Case 1-W, and both generations relatively prefer 3-C to 2-W. However, it does not imply that I_2 obtains more benefits than I_1 in Case 2-W or Case 3-C.

However, in Case 4-W, where a wage tax is used, there is no stimulation effect through taxation, and the negative effect of the high tax rate in the future due to the interest payment reduces utility depending on when generations were born. Since *EV(I)* is measured in comparison with the utility level in Case 1-W, where a wage tax is used to maintain a 90% level of the D-G ratio in a steady state, all generations prefer Case 1 to Case 4 when a wage tax is used due to the reason that a higher wage tax will be imposed in the future. However, when a consumption tax is used, for the generations born in relatively earlier periods, the negative effect of imposing a higher tax in the future is smaller than the positive effect of consumption taxation, and the generations born prior to late 2020 prefer Case 4 to Case 1 when a consumption tax is used.

Furthermore, when a consumption tax is used, only the generations born after year 2045 prefer about a zero D-G ratio (Case 3-C) in a steady state to a 90% steady state D-G ratio (Case 1-C). Since the generations born after 2035 prefer Case 3-C to Case 1-C when a wage tax is used, the difference in the way to finance the shortage results in the 10-year difference in generation on the evaluation of the government deficitpolicy.

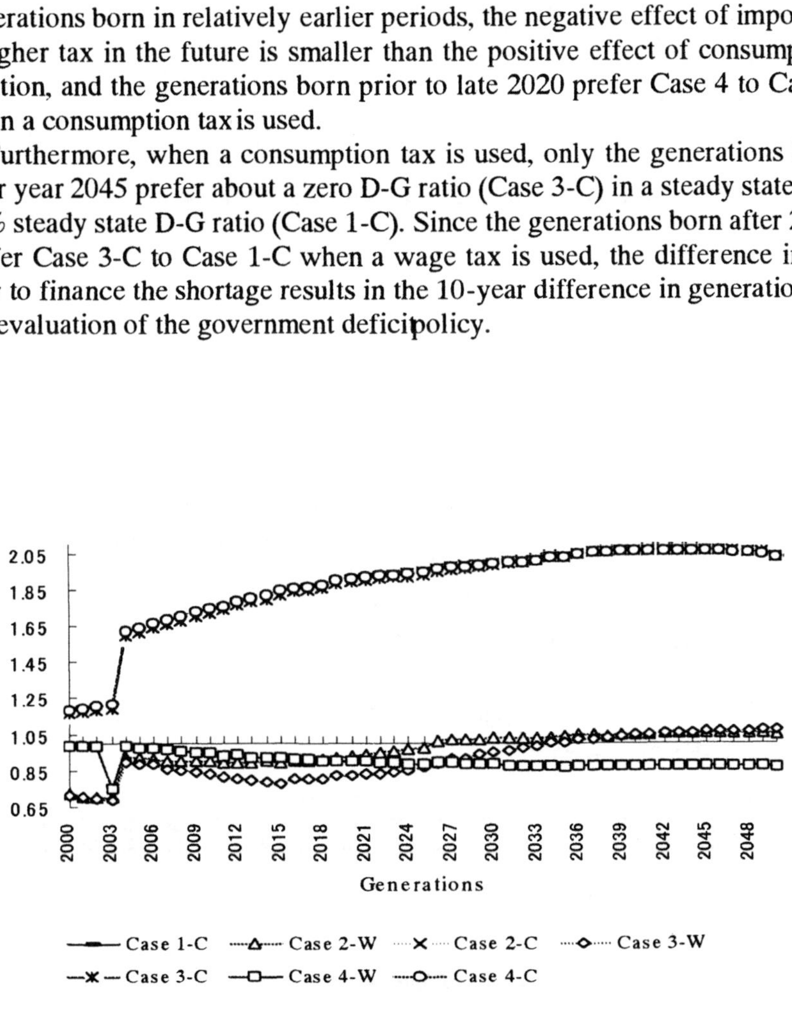

Figure4.

EV(Utility levels), benchmark: Case 1-W

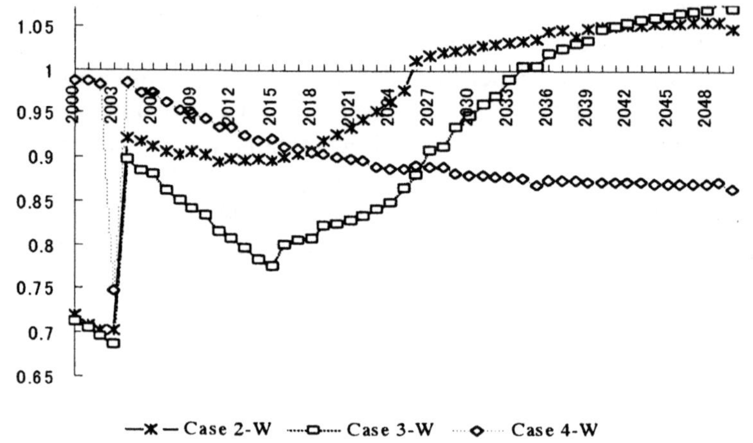

Figure4.1.

EV(Utility levels), with a wage tax, benchmark: Case 1 -W

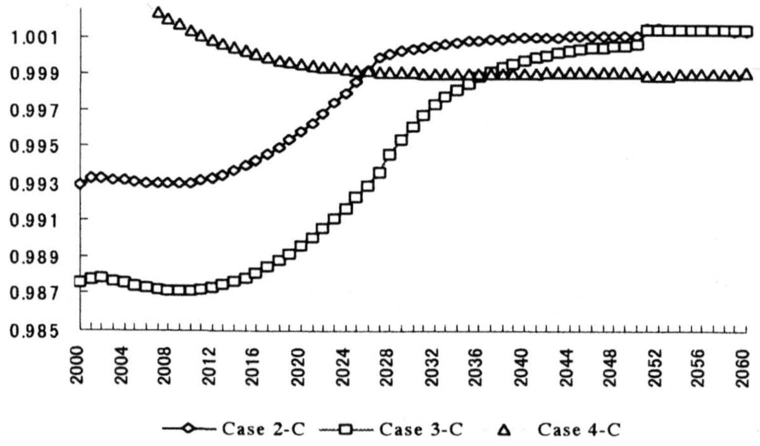

Figure 4.2.

EV(Utility levels), with a consumption tax, benchmark: Case 1-C

5. CONCLUDING REMARKS

This chapter has examined the effects of government deficits and public pension policies on tax burden, capital accumulation and economic welfare in the transition to an aging Japan by applying a simulated method in the expanded life cycle growth model.

The results obtained in this chapter are summarised as follows: First of all, outstanding future government deficits in Japan will increase the ratio of public to national income (Kokumin Hutanritsu: the P-N ratio) . The P-N ratio will increase up to 48.71% in year 2027 when a zero debt-GDP ratio (the D-G ratio) is achieved in a steady state (Case 3), and up to 50.00% in year 2044 when a 110% level of the D-G ratio is maintained in a steady state (Case 4). An increase in the P-N ratio (Kokumin Hutanritsu) in Case 3 is caused by a rapid increase in the tax rate associated with strong efforts to decrease government deficits, and thus the P-N ratio (Kokumin Hutanritsu) will finally decrease after the debts are paid off. However, an increase in the P-N ratio in Case 4 is caused by an increase in the tax rate to finance interest payment incurred from outstanding government debts, and the high P-N ratio is kept through time in Case 4.

Secondly, the trend increase in the P-N ratio can be mainly explained by the trend increase in the social security contribution ratio caused by an aging population in Japan.

Thirdly, a consumption tax is preferable to a wage tax in order to redeem outstanding government debts since a consumption tax has a positive effect on savings, thus resulting in capital accumulation being relatively stimulated.

Fourthly, when a wage tax is used to redeem outstanding future government deficits, a scenario to maintain a 110% level of the D-G ratio in a steady state is not preferred by all generations. However, when a consumption tax is used, this policy would be preferred by old generations to the policy under the scenario that the D-G ratio is maintained at a 90% level in a steady state.

Finally, a lower level of outstanding government debts in a steady state is more preferred by future generations. This is because a lower steady state level of outstanding government deficits is followed by an increase in the tax rate at a relatively earlier stage, and this implies that a relatively lower tax is imposed on future generations to finance interest payment incurred from the smaller amount of outstanding government debts

APPENDIX 1

For the utility maximization problem over time, Lagrange function is given such that:

$$L = U + \sum_{s=1}^{80} \lambda_s \{A_{s+1} - [[1 + (1 - \tau_r(t))r(t)]A_s$$
$$+ (1 - \tau_y(t) - \tau_p(t))w(t)e_s + b_s + a_s - (1 + \tau_c(t))C_s]\}$$
$$+ \sum_{s=1}^{80} \{\phi_{2s}(DY_s - C_s) + \phi_{1s}(C_s - C_{MIN})\}$$

and the first-order conditions are:

$$S_s(1+\delta)^{-(s-1)} C_s^{-1/\gamma} - \lambda_s PC(t) - \phi_{2s} + \phi_{1s} = 0$$
$$-\lambda_s + \lambda_{s+1} ARA(t) = 0$$
$$\phi_{2s}(DY_s - C_s) = 0$$
$$\phi_{1s}(C_s - C_{MIN}) = 0,$$

where

$$PC(t) = 1 + \tau_c(t),$$
$$ARA(t) = 1 + (1 - \tau_r(t))r(t).$$

and λ_S, ϕ_{1S} and ϕ_{2S} represent the Lagrange multipliers for (2), (3), and (4), respectively. The above first order conditions yield

$$C_s = \{ANC_s C_1^{-1/\gamma} + AOB_s\}^{-\gamma}.$$

where

$$ANB(t) = \frac{PC(t)}{PC(1)\prod_{t=1}^{80} ARA(t)}$$

$$ANC_s = \frac{ANB(t)S_1(1+\delta)^{(s-1)}}{S_s},$$

$$PC(t) = 1 + \tau_c(t),$$
$$ARA(t) = 1 + (1 - \tau_r(t))r(t),$$

and

$$AOB_s = \frac{(1+\delta)^{(s-1)}}{S_s} \times$$
$$\left\{ ANB(t) \left[\phi_{11} - \phi_{21} - PC(1) \sum_{s=2}^{80} \phi_{2s} DY_s \left(\prod_{t=1}^{s-1} ARA(t) \right) \right] + \phi_{2s} - \phi_{1s} \right\}$$

From (5), the optimal consumption behaviour of all ages can be derived, if the initial consumption level, C_1, is specified. And the savings level can be calculated from (2) and (5). To derive C_1, (5) is substituted into the life cycle budget constraint such that:

$$\sum \frac{PC(t)C_s}{\prod ARA\ (t)} = \sum \frac{(1-\tau_y(t)-\tau_p(t))w(t)e_s}{\prod ARA\ (t)} + \sum \frac{b_s}{\prod ARA\ (t)} + \sum \frac{a_s}{\prod ARA\ (t)}.$$

APPENDIX 2

(The D-G Ratios)
Future values of the debt-GDP ratio

	Case 1-W/C	Case 2-W/C	Case 3-W/C	Case 4-W/C
1967	7.57%	7.57%	7.57%	7.57%
1968	7.71%	7.71%	7.71%	7.71%
1969	7.61%	7.61%	7.61%	7.61%
1970	7.68%	7.68%	7.68%	7.68%
1975	17.29%	17.29%	17.29%	17.29%
1980	40.74%	40.74%	40.74%	40.74%
1985	54.62%	54.62%	54.62%	54.62%
1990	50.46%	50.46%	50.46%	50.46%
1995	65.01%	65.01%	65.01%	65.01%
2000	83.10%	75.59%	75.59%	80.95%
2005	87.19%	79.64%	79.64%	92.99%
2010	87.60%	79.19%	79.19%	100.48%
2015	87.64%	74.25%	74.25%	104.91%
2020	87.65%	64.81%	64.81%	107.45%
2025	87.65%	50.87%	50.87%	108.89%
2030	87.65%	44.66%	31.73%	109.70%
2035	87.65%	42.25%	20.43%	110.15%
2040	87.65%	40.68%	14.01%	110.41%
2045	87.65%	39.66%	10.1%	110.54%
2050	87.6%	38.97%	7.68%	110.62%
2055	87.65%	38.51%	6.05%	110.67%
2060	87.65%	38.20%	4.92%	110.69%

APPENDIX 3

(The R-N Ratios)
Future values of the ratio of public to national income (%)

	Case 1-W	Case 1-C	Case 2-W	Case 2-C
2000	35.42%	35.73%	36.42%	35.99%
2005	39.08%	36.71%	38.71%	36.34%
2010	40.43%	38.18%	40.68%	38.47%
2015	42.11%	39.76%	43.07%	40.78%
2020	44.05%	41.51%	45.63%	43.32%
2025	45.28%	42.53%	47.34%	45.06%
2030	46.20%	43.20%	45.46%	43.14%
2035	46.95%	43.67%	45.71%	43.34%
2040	47.65%	44.16%	45.98%	43.67%
2045	47.82%	44.44%	45.95%	43.83%
2050	47.50%	44.57%	45.62%	43.87%
2055	46.80%	44.59%	45.06%	43.83%
2060	45.99%	44.50%	44.38%	43.69%
	Case 3-W	Case 3-C	Case 4-W	Case 4-C
2000	36.42%	35.96%	35.41%	35.06%
2005	38.70%	36.31%	38.09%	34.67%
2010	40.67%	38.45%	40.16%	36.79%
2015	43.05%	40.74%	42.49%	38.85%
2020	45.63%	43.24%	44.94%	40.88%
2025	47.33%	44.95%	46.48%	42.06%
2030	47.69%	45.44%	47.69%	42.81%
2035	46.45%	44.32%	48.72%	43.34%
2040	45.98%	43.99%	49.69%	43.87%
2045	45.56%	43.81%	49.99%	44.18%
2050	45.07%	43.66%	49.53%	44.31%
2055	44.44%	43.50%	48.53%	44.34%
2060	43.77%	43.29%	47.50%	44.25%

APPENDIX 4

Future values of the social security contribution ratio

	Case 1-W	Case 1-C	Case 2-W	Case 2-C
2000	12.96%	12.07%	12.93%	11.98%
2005	13.74%	12.39%	13.71%	12.25%
2010	14.22%	12.99%	14.17%	12.88%
2015	14.97%	13.72%	14.88%	13.50%
2020	16.42%	15.03%	16.26%	14.76%
2025	17.39%	15.87%	17.13%	15.50%
2030	17.97%	16.34%	17.64%	15.94%
2035	18.15%	16.46%	17.76%	16.03%
2040	17.97%	16.29%	17.51%	15.84%
2045	17.73%	16.14%	17.22%	15.67%
2050	17.44%	16.04%	16.84%	15.55%
2055	17.11%	16.02%	16.43%	15.52%
2060	16.75%	16.04%	16.00%	15.52%
	Case 3-W	Case 3-C	Case 4-W	Case 4-C
2000	12.93%	11.95%	13.43%	12.13%
2005	13.70%	12.23%	14.25%	12.46%
2010	14.17%	12.85%	14.77%	13.09%
2015	14.88%	13.46%	15.56%	13.87%
2020	16.26%	14.68%	17.08%	15.20%
2025	17.13%	15.40%	18.11%	16.07%
2030	17.56%	15.73%	18.73%	16.55%
2035	17.62%	15.77%	18.93%	16.68%
2040	17.34%	15.56%	18.74%	16.51%
2045	17.00%	15.37%	18.51%	16.37%
2050	16.58%	15.24%	18.26%	16.27%
2055	16.10%	15.19%	17.96%	16.27%
2060	15.65%	15.18%	17.61%	16.30%

REFERENCES

Altig, D, A Auerbach, L Kotlikoff, K Smetters, and J Walliser, 2001, Simulating fundamental tax reform in the United States, *American Economic Review* 91, 574-595.

Asako, K et al, 1993, The Theory of 'Tax smoothing' and the behaviour of Japan's public debt (Nihon no Zaisei Unei to Ijitenkan no Shigen Haibun), *Economic Analysis* 131, Economic Planning Agency of Japan (in Japanese).

Aso, Y, 1997, Shoshika taisaku wa nenkin hutan wo keigen suruka, *Jinko Mondai Kenkyu*, 53-54 (in Japanese).

Aso, Y, 1998, Shoshika no eikyo, *Financial Review* 47, 154-172 (in Japanese).

Atoda, N. and R. R. Kato, 1993, Savings and taxation in an aging Japan (Koreika shakai ni okeru chochiku to zeisei), *Tezukaya University Discussion Paper* J-034, Tezukaya University (in Japanese).

Auerbach, A and L. J. Kotlikoff, 1987, *Dynamic Fiscal Policy*, Cambridge Univ Press.

Doi, T. and T. Nakazato, 1998, Kokusai to chihousai no jizoku kanousei: Chiho zaisei taisaku no seiji keizaigaku, *Financial Review* 47, 76-105 (in Japanese).

Hatta, T. and N. Oguchi, 1999, *Nenkin Kaikakuron: Tsumitate Houshiki ni Ikoseyo*, Nihon Keizai Shinbunsya (in Japanese).

Homma, M., N. Atoda, Y. Iwamoto and F. Ohtake, 1987, Nenkin: Koureika shakai to nenkin seido, in Hamada, Horiuchi and Kuroda eds., *Nihon Keizai no Macro Bunseki*, Tokyo Univ Press (in Japanese).

Iwamoto, Y., 1990, Nenkin seisaku to isan kodo, *Kikan Shakai Hosyo Kenkyu* 25, 388-411 (in Japanese).

Iwamoto, Y., R. R. Kato and M. Hidaka, 1991, An aging population and public pension scheme in Japan (Jinko koureika to kouteki nenkin), *Kikan Shakai Hosyo kenkyu* 27, 285-294 (in Japanese).

Iwamoto, Y., R. R. Kato and M. Hidaka, 1993, Public pension and an aging population, *Review of Social Policy* 2, 1-10.

Kato, R. R., 1998, Transition to an aging Japan: public pension, savings and capital taxation, *Journal of the Japanese and International Economies* 12, 204-231.

Kato, R. R., 2000, Wagakuni no koreika iko to zaisei akaji (Transition to an aging society and government deficits in Japan), in T. Ihori, R.R. Kato, H. Nakano, T. Nakazato, T. Doi, and S. Sato, *Economic Analysis of Budget Deficits, Economic Analysis, Shiten Series* 16, 69-138 (in Japanese).

Kato, R. R., 2001, Government deficit, public investment and public capital in the transition to an aging Japan, *mimeo*.

Kawagoe, M., 2000, Nihon ni towareru zaisei saiken heno michi, *Ronso: Toyo Keizai*, 173-178, Toyo Keizai (in Japanese)

Chapter 6

Public Works

1. ECONOMIC IMPLICATION OF PUBLIC WORKS

As explained in chapter 1, in 1998 the Japanese government abandoned the fiscal reconstruction plan and increased issues of government bonds and spending on public works. Spending on public works has been very high in Japan among developed countries. The ratio of general government fixed capital formation to GDP amounted to 8% in 1998, compared with 1 to 3% in other industrial countries.

Economic implications of public works may be evaluated in two ways; the long-run supply side effect and the short-run demand side effect. In Japan the demand side effect has been regarded as the top priority since fiscal policy has mainly been employed so as to stimulate aggregate demand during recession. However, it is widely recognized that the multiplier effect of public works has become very low in recent years, and hence the efficacy of stimulating aggregate demand by using public works is controversial. The resulting cost is a huge increase in government deficitin the 1990s.

In the standard Keynesian framework, public works stimulate the private consumption-saving behavior by generating effective demand, while the supply side benefit of the public works is irrelevant. On the contrary, in the neoclassical framework where people are concerned with the costs and the supply side benefits of public spending, the public works may affect consumption-saving behavior in a different way from the Keynesian theory. Only if public works really produce net benefits in the future, can they stimulate private consumption as well as enhancing economic welfare. Therefore, it is more and more important to consider the efficiency of public capital provision. In recent years, it is widely believed in Japan that the aggregate level of public capital is sufficient. However, it is also well recognized that there may be a shortage of public capital in some areas such as public works in the urban area.

In this chapter, firstly, we investigates macroeconomic implications of the long-run supply side effect of public works on private consumption by incorporating the benefits of public works explicitly into the utility function and the production function. The impact of an unexpected increase in public investment on private consumption is smaller in recent years. This empirical result may suggest that the total level of public capital may be sufficient in recent years, but does not exclude the possibility that some public capital goods are still too low compared with the efficient level. Therefore, we investigate the efficiency of disaggregated public capital for Japan by estimating and testing the efficient allocation conditions using Hansen (1982)'s generalized method of moments (GMM).

2. SIZE OF PUBLIC SPENDING

Ihori (1987) investigated the impact of anticipated and unanticipated public spending on private consumption. Namely, if public spending G is initially too little, unanticipated government expenditures have a relatively more expansionary effect on private consumption than anticipated government expenditures, and vice versa. Based on these theoretical considerations, the relative effects of anticipated expansion and unanticipated expansion tell us the discrepancy between actual and optimal government expenditures.

An intuitive explanation is as follows. If G is initially too little, an unanticipated increase in public consumption G_t raises welfare when the tax burden of public spending is entirely levied on private consumption in the same period. If the individual anticipates this policy change in advance, it is desirable for him (or her) to transfer private consumption from period t to period t-1. By doing so, the Euler equation is restored. If he (or she) does not anticipate this change in advance, it is impossible to transfer private consumption from period t to period t-1. Therefore, unanticipated government action will raise private consumption at that time more than anticipated government action.

Ihori (1987) provided some empirical evidence of a discrepancy between actual and optimal government consumption in two ways for the Japanese economy. First, he used a direct approach to estimate a parameter of evaluation, which exploits restrictions placed on the data by the Euler equation. Second, he used an indirect approach to estimate the relationship between the optimal size and the actual size of government spending. His empirical analysis provided the finding that the level of government spending was regarded as too little in the 1960s, but is regarded as too much in recent years for the Japanese economy.

3. PUBLIC INVESTMENT AND PRIVATE CONSUMPTION

This chapter develops Ihori (1987)'s framework and investigates the impact of public investment on private consumption and economic welfare by explicitly incorporating the benefits of public investment into the utility function and the production function respectively[1].

3.1 Public investment in utility function

First, we explicitly consider the benefits of public works The representative individual's utility function is given by

$$U = \sum_{t=0}^{\infty} \left(\frac{1}{1+\rho} \right)^t u(C_t^*) , \tag{1}$$

where C_t* denotes the level of "effective" consumption in period t and ρ is the discount rate. Effective consumption is taken to be a function of private consumption expenditure, C_t, and the benefit of public works G_{t-1} which is accumulated in the preceding period:

$$C_t^* = C_t + \mu(G_{t-1}) , \quad \mu' > 0, \ \mu'' < 0. \tag{2}$$

Here μ' may be regarded as the marginal rate of substitution between private consumption and government investment. The benefit μ is increasing with government expenditure on public works G. However, the greater the level of government expenditures, the smaller marginal utility a unit of government goods and services yields in terms of private consumption.

The effective lifetime budget equation is written as

$$\sum_{t=0}^{\infty} \left(\frac{1}{1+r} \right)^t \{C_t + \mu(G_{t-1})\} = \sum_{t=0}^{\infty} \left(\frac{1}{1+r} \right)^t \{Y_t - G_t + \mu(G_{t-1})\} + A_0 ,$$

[1] See also Ihori and Kondo (1998) and Kondo and Ihori (1999).

$$\lim_{t\to\infty}\left(\frac{1}{1+r}\right)^t A_0 = 0 \tag{3}$$

where Y_t is endogenously given labor income in period t , r is the rate of interest and A_0 is initial assets. As in chapter 4 we assume that the discount rate ρ is equal to the interest rate r and labor income Y_t is constant over time. The sequence of the government expenditure on public works $\{G_t\}_{t=0}^{\infty}$ is taken as given for the individual.

The efficient size of public investment G^* is hence given by

$$1+\rho = \mu'(G^*). \tag{4}$$

We now consider how an unexpected permanent increase in the level of public investment affects private consumption. For simplicity, we focus on the following case. By period -1, public investment has been kept at the constant level $\overline{G}$ but after period 0 it is raised to be $\overline{G}+dG$. The change is not expected until period 0. The induced changes in private consumption after period 0 are written as

$$\frac{dC_0}{dG} = -1 + \frac{\mu'(\overline{G})}{1+\rho}, \tag{5}$$

$$\frac{dC_t}{dG} = -1 - \rho\frac{\mu'(\overline{G})}{1+\rho}, \quad t = 1,2,3,\cdots. \tag{6}$$

Remember that public works do not produce benefits until the next period. Namely, an increase in public investment only brings the cost in the initial period. However, individuals may adjust their consumption path considering the future benefits of public investment. Therefore, initial consumption can be changed.

Does consumption in period 0 increase? From (4) and (5) we obtain

$$\overline{G} < G^* \Rightarrow \frac{dC_0}{dG} = -1 + \frac{\mu'(\overline{G})}{1+\rho} > 0,$$

$$\overline{G} = G^* \Rightarrow \frac{dC_0}{dG} = -1 + \frac{\mu'(\overline{G})}{1+\rho} = 0,$$

$$\overline{G} > G^* \Rightarrow \frac{dC_0}{dG} = -1 + \frac{\mu'(\overline{G})}{1+\rho} < 0. \tag{7}$$

That is, private consumption in period 0 is stimulated when public capital is too little in period 0, and vice versa. Namely, the increase in public works will stimulate private consumption in the same period if and only if public capital is regarded as too little initially.

The reason is as follows. If $\overline{G} < G^*$, an increase in G will raise the right-hand-side of equation (3). Therefore, individuals increase their effective consumption C^* from period 0. However, they can not get the larger benefits of public capital until period 1. To keep their effective consumption level smoother, they increase their private consumption in period 0 by decreasing private consumption from period 1. The result is presented in Figure 1(i).

On the other hand, if $\overline{G} > G^*$, an increase in G will reduce the right-hand-side of equation (3). Therefore individuals decrease their effective consumption C^*. As the matter of course, they must decrease their private consumption too. The result is described in Figure 1(ii). Finally, at the efficient size of public investment $\overline{G} = G^*$, a marginal change of public investment does not affect private consumption

3.2 Public investment in production function

Next, following Kondo and Ihori (1999), we incorporate the benefits of public capital into the production function in place of the utility function. The individual's utility function and lifetime budget equation are respectively written as

$$U = \sum_{t=0}^{\infty}\left(\frac{1}{1+\rho}\right)^t u(C_t), \tag{8}$$

$$\sum_{t=0}^{\infty}\left(\frac{1}{1+r}\right)^t C_t = \sum_{t=0}^{\infty}\left(\frac{1}{1+r}\right)^t \{Y(G_{t-1}) - G_t\} + A_0\ ,\ \lim_{t\to\infty}\left(\frac{1}{1+r}\right)^t A_t = 0, \tag{9}$$

where

$$Y' > 0, Y'' < 0.$$

It is assumed that public investment produces public capital in the next period and it has the positiveeffect on output.

Is it realistic to assume that public capital is productive? Aschauer (1989) estimated an aggregate production function and studied the potential effects of public capital on output. Batina (1998) found interesting evidence of cointegration properties among aggregate output, labor, private capital and public capital in the U.S. economy. Iwamoto (1990), Asako et.al. (1994), Mitsui and Ohta (1995), Yoshino and Nakano (1996) and Doi (1998) empirically study the productivity of public capital in Japan and commonly conclude that public capital was productive.

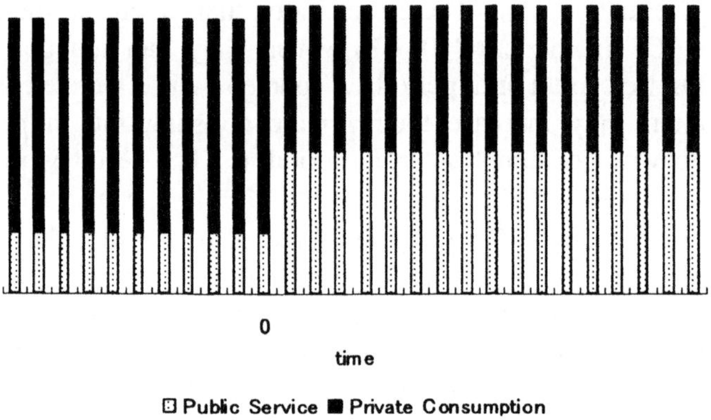

Case (i)

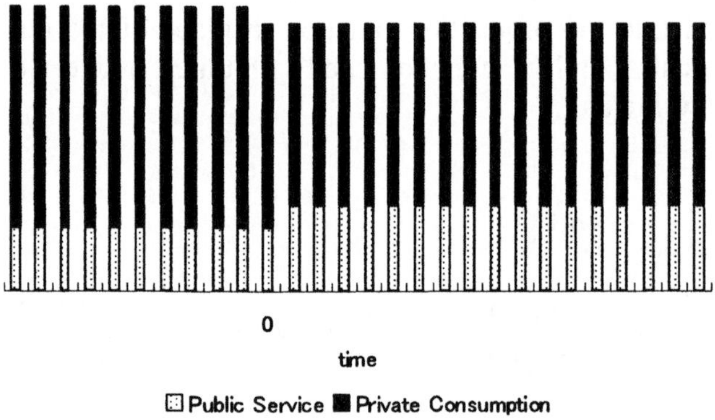

case (ii)

Figure1. Dynamics of efficient consumption

The efficient size of public investment G^* is hence given by

$$1+\rho = Y'(G^*). \tag{10}$$

We now consider how an unexpected permanent increase in the level of public investment affects private consumption. The impact on private consumption after period 0 are written as

$$\frac{dC_t}{dG} = -1 + \frac{Y'(\overline{G})}{1+\rho}, \quad t = 0,1,2,\cdots. \tag{11}$$

From (10) and (11), we obtain

$$\begin{aligned}
\overline{G} < G^* &\Rightarrow \frac{dC_t}{dG} = -1 + \frac{Y'(\overline{G})}{1+\rho} > 0, \\
\overline{G} = G^* &\Rightarrow \frac{dC_t}{dG} = -1 + \frac{Y'(\overline{G})}{1+\rho} = 0, \\
\overline{G} > G^* &\Rightarrow \frac{dC_t}{dG} = -1 + \frac{Y'(\overline{G})}{1+\rho} < 0.
\end{aligned} \tag{12}$$

That is, the increase in public works will stimulate private consumption in the same period if and only if public capital is too little initially. Intuition is almost the same as in section 6.4.

These analytical results could explain the reason why private consumption was not stimulated much by the increase in public works in recent years in Japan. Namely, the total level of public capital may not be too little in recent years. Keeping this possibility in mind, we can measure the effects of the change in public investmenton private consumption.

3.3 Measuring the effects of public investment on private consumption

In this chapter, we have derived theoretically the efficient size of public capital and showed that an increase in public works stimulates private consumption in the same period if and only if the public capital is initially too little. Here we now measure the effect of the change in public investmenton private consumption for the Japanese economy.

Ihori and Kondo (1998) investigated the effect of public investment on private consumption by estimating the consumption function. We found that the impact of public investment on private consumption was large in the 1960s but has become lower since 1980. However, some of the results were not statistically significant and in these regressions the adaptive expectation mechanism was assumed.

In Kondo and Ihori (1999), we estimate the following VAR model for the period FY1958-1995:

$$\Delta X_t = \Phi_1 \Delta X_{t-1} + \cdots + \Phi_k \Delta X_{t-k} + \varepsilon_t \tag{13}$$

where $X_t=(C_t,\ G_t)'$, $\varepsilon_t=(\varepsilon_t^C,\ \varepsilon_t^G)'$ and each of the Φ_t is a (2×2) matrix of parameters. C_t and G_t are private consumption and public investment respectively. As for C_t and G_t, we use private final consumption expenditure and general government's gross domestic fixed capital formation in "Annual Report on National Accounts" respectively. The effect of an unexpected change in public investment on private consumption can be estimated as the impulse response of C_t to ε_t^G.[2]

In Table 1 we list the estimates of the VAR model incorporating a lag length equal to two. In Table 1, F-value is the one used for the test for the Granger causality between G and C. The causality from G to C is significant in the whole sample period. It is noteworthy that the causality is strong in the period 1958-1995, but it fades out in recent years.

The impulse responses are depicted in Figure 2. In the whole sample period, private consumption is stimulated by an unexpected increase in public investment. Moreover, it is noteworthy that the impact is large in the period 1958-1975 but it is small in recent years.

These evidences tend to suggest that the total level of public capital may be sufficient in recent years. Hence, a further increase in public works would depress private consumption. Iwamoto (1990), Asako et.al. (1994), Mitsui and Ohta (1995), Yoshino and Nakano (1996) and Doi (1998) conclude that the productivity of public capital has declined recently in Japan. Otto and Voss (1998) and Kitasaka (1999) characterized the efficient allocation conditions of both private and public capital and examined whether these conditions were rejected by the data in Australia and in Japan respectively using GMM.[3] Kitasaka (1999) concluded that the stock of Japanese public capital goods was efficiently provided at the aggregate level. Their conclusions are all consistent with our results here. However, even

[2] Preceding the VAR analysis, it must be checked whether the data is stationary in first difference. The augmented Dickey-Fuller (ADF) test statistics of private consumption and public investment are -2.82 and -1.49 respectively, so we could not reject the hypothesis that there exists a unit root. We must test for the cointegration relationship using Engle-Granger's procedure too. The ADF test statistics is –1.72, so the cointegration does not exist. Therefore, the VAR model can be estimated safely.

[3] Such an approach has often been employed to estimate and test the conditions for intertemporal efficiency in the asset pricing literature (e.g Hansen and Singleton, 1982 and Cochrane, 1991). In recent years, it is applied to examine the dynamic efficiency of public investment policy.

though public capital has been sufficiently provided in the aggregate level, it does not necessarily mean that efficiency is attained at the disaggregated level. In the remainder of this chapter, following Ihori and Kondo (2001), we consider the efficiency of disaggregated public capitafor Japan.

Table 1. The estimates of a VAR

	⊿G	⊿C
Constant	325.72 (0.49)	3528.80 (3.43)***
⊿G(-1)	0.44 (2.62)**	0.58 (2.24)**
⊿G(-2)	-0.13 (-0.73)	-0.57 (-2.09)**
⊿C(-1)	-0.16 (-1.47)	0.62 (3.79)***
⊿C(-2)	0.22 (2.25)**	-0.17(-1.11)
F-value	2.60*	3.37**

1958-1995

	⊿G	⊿C
Constant	-111.58 (-0.18)	1857.98(1.78)*
⊿G(-1)	0.61 (2.90)**	1.79 (5.23)***
⊿G(-2)	-0.62 (-1.81)*	-0.81 (-1.44)
⊿C(-1)	-0.03 (-0.20)	0.43 (1.61)
⊿C(-2)	0.23 (2.27)**	0.10 (0.62)
F-value	3.29*	14.12***

1958-1975

	⊿G	⊿C
Constant	273.79 (0.21)	4706.17 (2.73)**
⊿G(-1)	0.38 (1.47)	0.24 (0.68)
⊿G(-2)	-.0.05 (-0.20)	-0.45 (-1.27)
⊿C(-1)	-0.14 (-0.80)	0.59 (2.40)**
⊿C(-2)	0.22 (1.28)	-0.26 (-1.11)
F-value	0.85	0.82

1976-1995

*** denotes rejection at the 1% significance level, ** at the 5 % and * at the 10%.

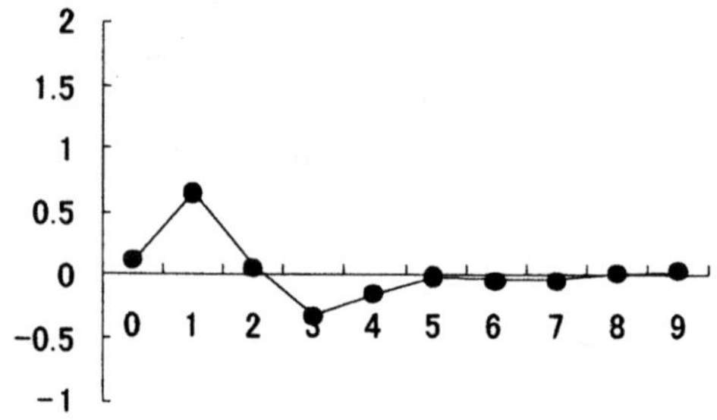

1958-1995

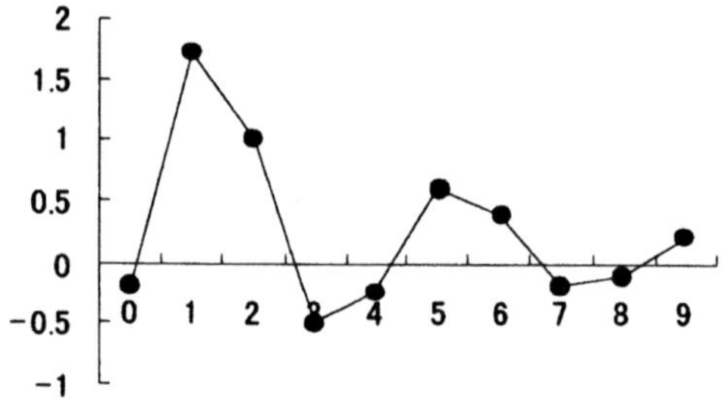

1958-1975

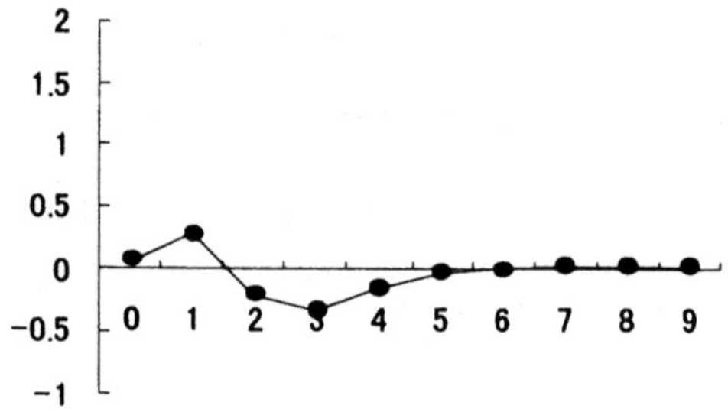

1976-1995

Figure 2. Impulse response of C to G

4. EFFICIENCY OF DISAGGREGATED PUBLIC CAPITAL PROVISION

4.1 Derivations of testable conditions

Firstly, we derive efficiency conditions of private and public capital goods provision. Then, we estimate the parameters in these conditions using GMM and examine whether the efficient provision hypothesis is rejected by an overidentification test statistic. This procedure provides useful information about which types of capital goods are efficiently provided. However, it does not provide information about whether the other public capital goods are too small or not compared with the efficient level. Therefore, we estimate an aggregate production function, too. The results may provide some information about the allocation of the public capital goods, some of which are judged to be inefficiently provided by the GMM estimates.

Efficient provision conditions of private and public capital goods are obtained by solving the following maximization problem:

$$\textbf{MAX} \quad E_t\left[\sum_{\tau=t}^{\infty}\left(\frac{1}{1+\rho}\right)^{\tau-t} u(C_\tau)\right], \tag{14}$$

subject to

$$PK_{t+1}+\sum_{i=1}^{n} GK_{t+1}^{i}=Y(\mathbf{GK}_t,PK_t,L_t)-C_t+(1-\delta_{PK})PK_t+(1-\delta_{GK})\sum_{i=1}^{n} GK_t^{i} \; . \tag{15}$$

In (14), ρ denotes the discount rate and C_t denotes private consumption. $u(\ )$ is the instantaneous utility function. In (15), Y, **GK**, PK and L denote aggregate output, a vector of public capital stocks, the private capital stock, and the labor input, respectively. Also, δ_{PK} and δ_{GK} denote the depreciation rates of private and public capital goods. The public capital vector **GK** represents n types of public capital goods:

$$\mathbf{GK}_t = (GK_t^1\, GK_t^2 \cdots GK_t^n)\,.$$

The efficiency conditions are as follows (Euler equations):

$$E_t\left[\left(\frac{1}{1+\rho}\right)\left(\frac{u'(C_{t+1})}{u'(C_t)}\right)\left(\frac{\partial F(\mathbf{GK}_{t+1}, PK_{t+1}, L_{t+1})}{\partial PK_{t+1}}+(1-\delta_{PK})\right)-1\right]=0, \quad (16)$$

$$E_t\left[\left(\frac{1}{1+\rho}\right)\left(\frac{u'(C_{t+1})}{u'(C_t)}\right)\left(\frac{\partial F(\mathbf{GK}_{t+1}, PK_{t+1}, L_{t+1})}{\partial GK^i_{t+1}}+(1-\delta_{GK})\right)-1\right]=0,$$

$$i=1,2,\cdots,n. \quad (17)$$

These $n+1$ conditions imply, roughly, that in each period there should be no differences among the returns of all the capital goods and that in the long run they should be equal to the individual's discount rate, too, as discussed by Arrow and Kurtz (1970).

We assumed that the relative prices for investment goods to output or consumption goods are constant. However, as we will see later, that is not the case in Japan. The public investment goods have become more expensive than aggregate output over time. This reflects the adjustment costs associated with the installation of capital goods. Including relative prices for investment goods in our model, we modify the conditions (16) and (17) as

$$E_t\left[\left(\frac{1}{1+\rho}\right)\left(\frac{u'(C_{t+1})}{u'(C_t)}\right)\left(\frac{1}{p_t}\right)\left(\frac{\partial F(\mathbf{GK}_{t+1}, PK_{t+1}, L_{t+1})}{\partial PK_{t+1}}+(1-\delta_{PK})p_{t+1}\right)-1\right]=0, \quad (18)$$

$$E_t\left[\left(\frac{1}{1+\rho}\right)\left(\frac{u'(C_{t+1})}{u'(C_t)}\right)\left(\frac{1}{p^i_t}\right)\left(\frac{\partial F(\mathbf{GK}_{t+1}, PK_{t+1}, L_{t+1})}{\partial GK^i_{t+1}}+(1-\delta_{GK})p^i_{t+1}\right)-1\right]=0,$$

$$i=1,2,\cdots,n \quad (19)$$

where p_t and p_t^i are relative prices for private and public investment goods to aggregate output respectively.

4.2 Empirical evidence

The data sources we use are summarized in the Appendix. We sum up disaggregated public capital goods to the following five components:

Group 1: Roads, harbors and airports
(consists of 3 types of public capital goods)

Group 2: Railways
(consists of 3 types of public capital goods)

Group 3: Postal service, telephone and telegraph
(consists of 2 types of public capital goods)

Group 4: Agriculture-related public capitals and fishing ports

(consists of 2 types of public capital goods)

Group 5: Measures for flood control and conservation of forests (consists of 3 types of public capital goods).

Figure 3 shows that the series Y/PK and Y/GK^i (i=1,...,5) may exhibit nonstationary behavior[4] and Figure 4 shows that investment goods have been more expensive than aggregate output. The model without adjustment costs of investments is less realistic than the model with adjustment costs. Therefore, we focus on the efficiency conditions of public capital provision (18) and (19) derived from the model with adjustment costs.

To transform (18) and (19) into testable equations, we specify the production function and utility functionas the following:

$$Y_t = PK_t^{\beta} GK_{1t}^{\gamma_1} GK_{2t}^{\gamma_2} GK_{3t}^{\gamma_3} GK_{4t}^{\gamma_4} GK_{5t}^{\gamma_5} L_t^{\phi}. \tag{20}$$

$$u(C_t) = \frac{C_t^{1-\sigma} - 1}{1-\sigma}, \tag{21}$$

where σ is the coefficient of relative risk aversion and is non-negative. With these specifications, (18) and (19) are rewritten as

$$E_t\left[\left(\frac{1}{1+\rho}\right)\left(\frac{C_{t+1}}{C_t}\right)^{-\sigma}\left(\frac{1}{p_t}\right)\left(\beta\frac{Y_{t+1}}{PK_{t+1}} + (1-\delta_{PK})p_{t+1}\right) - 1\right] = 0\,, \tag{22}$$

$$E_t\left[\left(\frac{1}{1+\rho}\right)\left(\frac{C_{t+1}}{C_t}\right)^{-\sigma}\left(\frac{1}{p_t^i}\right)\left(\gamma_i\frac{Y_{t+1}}{GK_{t+1}^i} + (1-\delta_{GK})p_{t+1}^i\right) - 1\right] = 0$$

$$i = 1,2,\cdots,5\;. \tag{23}$$

These conditions mean thatthe 6 dimension random vector defined as

$$u_{t+1} = \begin{pmatrix} \left(\frac{1}{1+\rho}\right)\left(\frac{C_{t+1}}{C_t}\right)^{-\sigma}\left(\frac{1}{p_t}\right)\left(\beta\frac{Y_{t+1}}{PK_{t+1}} + (1-\delta_{PK})p_{t+1}\right) - 1 \\ \left(\frac{1}{1+\rho}\right)\left(\frac{C_{t+1}}{C_t}\right)^{-\sigma}\left(\frac{1}{p_t^1}\right)\left(\gamma_1\frac{Y_{t+1}}{GK_{t+1}^1} + (1-\delta_{GK})p_{t+1}^1\right) - 1 \\ \vdots \\ \left(\frac{1}{1+\rho}\right)\left(\frac{C_{t+1}}{C_t}\right)^{-\sigma}\left(\frac{1}{p_t^5}\right)\left(\gamma_5\frac{Y_{t+1}}{GK_{t+1}^5} + (1-\delta_{GK})p_{t+1}^5\right) - 1 \end{pmatrix}$$

[4] For these series the hypotheses of a unit root can not be rejected even at the critical value of 20%.

should be uncorrelated with any information available at time t:

$$E(u_{t+1} \otimes I_t) = 0, \tag{24}$$

where I_t is the l dimension information set. These $6 \times l$ unconditional moment conditions are suitable for GMM, with which we estimate the parameters. However, we will focus on the estimation of only the production parameters: $\theta = (\beta, \gamma_1, \cdots, \gamma_5)$.

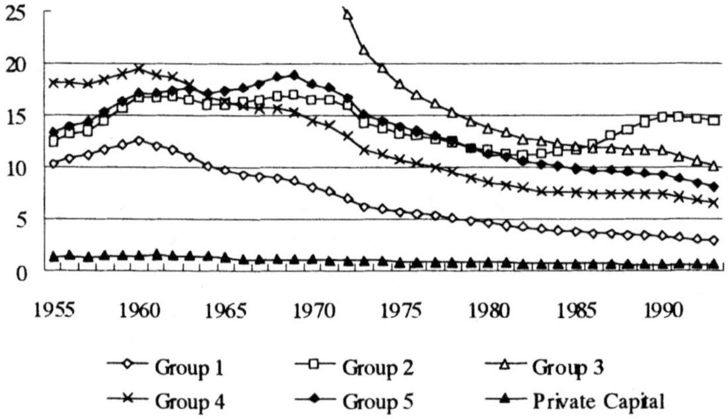

Figure 3. Output-capital rates

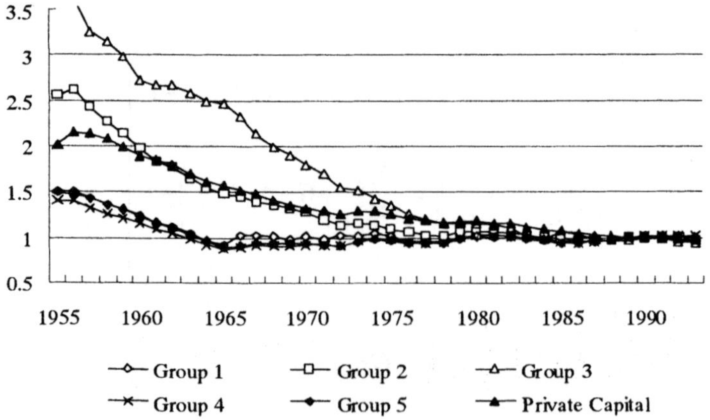

Figure 4. Relative prices of investment goods

Under the hypothesis that condition (24) is correct, Hansen's J-statistic is distributed as $\chi^2(6l-6)$. Then it can be used to test the validity of the model. However, a plausible conjecture is that not all capital goods are efficiently provided. Namely, (22) and only some of (23) will hold. Therefore, we analyze which public goods are efficiently provided changing the combinations of the public capital goods put into the GMM.

Before turning to GMM, we examine whether the variables included in equations (22) and (23) have unit roots by the Augmented-Dickey-Fuller (ADF) unit root test by estimating the regression

$$\Delta x_t = \lambda + \mu\, t + \phi_0 x_{t-1} + \sum_{j=1}^{m} \phi_j \Delta x_{t-j},$$

where x_t is a variable included in the efficiency conditions of public capital goods. Then we test the null hypotheses of a unit root that $\phi_0 = 0$ and that $\mu = 0$ and $\phi_0 = 0$. The results are presented in Table 2. For $Y_{t+1}/G_{t+1}^{\,2}/p_t^{\,2}$ and $Y_{t+1}/G_{t+1}^{\,3}/p_t^{\,3}$ the null hypotheses of a unit root cannot be rejected. It is well known that the GMM will not provide efficient estimates when nonstationary series are included. Moreover, we cannot say that such capital goods are efficiently provided from a theoretical point of view as discussed earlier. The returns of the capital goods are expected to converge to the households' discount rate in the long run as long as they are on the optimal accumulation path. The returns of the capital goods with unit roots violate such a condition. Therefore, we estimate (22) and (23) with respect to the three types of public capital (i=1, 4, 5).

We focus on the production parameters. Thus, as Otto and Voss (1998), we set the particular values for the other parameters. We set the discount rate ρ and the coefficient of relative risk aversion at 0.04 per annum and 2 respectively. We also set the depreciation rate of private capital goods δ_{PK} and that of public capital goods δ_{GK} at 0.06 and 0.04 per annum respectively. We include one and two lags of the following, C_{t+1}/C_t, $Y_{t+1}/PK_{t+1}/p_t$, $Y_{t+1}/G_{t+1}^{\,1}/p_t^{\,1}$, $Y_{t+1}/G_{t+1}^{\,4}/p_t^{\,4}$, $Y_{t+1}/G_{t+1}^{\,5}/p_t^{\,5}$ and a constant in instrumental variables set.

The estimation results are presented in Table 3. For each of the cases (i)-(vii), the efficiency conditions of public capital goods imposed by the model are supported by Hansen's J-statistic except for case (iv). In addition, we obtain a positive and significant estimate of the parameters.

Table 2. Univariate statistics and the results of the unit root tests

x_t	Mean	Std. Dev.	Maxi -mum	Mini -mum	t -statistics	F -statistics
C_{t+1}/C_t	1.048	0.028	1.097	0.999	-3.422*	5.930*
$Y_{t+1}/PK_{t+1}/p_t$	0.730	0.081	0.866	0.610	-3.480*	8.338**
$Y_{t+1}/GK^1_{t+1}/p^1_t$	6.430	2.663	10.636	2.854	-3.307*	6.016*
$Y_{t+1}/GK^2_{t+1}/p^2_t$	11.670	2.275	14.930	5.536	-2.633	4.069
$Y_{t+1}/GK^3_{t+1}/p^3_t$	15.107	3.654	22.899	10.893	-2.669	3.569
$Y_{t+1}/GK^4_{t+1}/p^4_t$	12.077	4.290	18.538	6.478	-3.252*	5.789*
$Y_{t+1}/GK^5_{t+1}/p^5_t$	13.663	3.870	20.214	8.016	-3.073	6.308*
p_{t+1}/p_t	0.978	0.017	1.022	0.946	-4.767***	11.436***
p^1_{t+1}/p^1_t	0.991	0.038	1.117	0.925	-3.553**	6.337*
p^2_{t+1}/p^2_t	0.975	0.029	1.039	0.922	-4.255***	9.202**
p^3_{t+1}/p^3_t	0.966	0.037	1.105	0.913	-4.997***	12.548***
p^4_{t+1}/p^4_t	0.993	0.030	1.053	0.936	-3.521*	6.298*
p^5_{t+1}/p^5_t	0.991	0.032	1.052	0.928	-3.610**	6.598*

Notes: Sample is 1957-1993. The 1, 5 and 10% critical values are indicated by ***, ** and * respectively.

Table 3. GMM results for efficiency conditions

	(i)	(ii)	(iii)	(iv)
β	0.2956*** (16.8525)	0.2909*** (16.7039)	0.2837*** (16.1723)	0.2877*** (16.5800)
γ_1	0.0278*** (18.9323)			0.0269*** (18.0375)
γ_4		0.0145*** (17.1886)		0.0141*** (16.4010)
γ_5			0.0123*** (10.8789)	
J-statistics	46.8082	42.4020	41.5363	68.4726*
p-value	0.107	0.214	0.242	0.089

	(v)	(vi)	(vii)
β	0.2767*** (15.7841)	0.2705*** (15.7772)	0.2673*** (15.7888)
γ_1	0.0262*** (17.5288)		0.02535*** (16.8233)
γ_4		0.0133*** (15.6698)	0.01295*** (15.0224)
γ_5	0.0116*** (10.2963)	0.0111*** (10.2855)	0.0108*** (10.0921)
J-statistics	67.4896	62.3072	85.8559
p-value	0.103	0.205	0.127

Notes: Sample is 1957-1992. The 1, 5 and 10 % critical values are indicated by ***, ** and * respectively. Hansen's J-statistics obeys χ^2 under the null hypothesis that the capital goods included in the estimation are efficiently provided.

With the estimates in case (vii), we calculate the returns of capital goods:

$$(1/p_t)(\hat{\beta}Y_{t+1}/PK_{t+1}+p_{t+1}(1-\delta_{PK}))$$

and

$$(1/p_t^i)(\hat{\gamma}_i Y_{t+1}/GK_{t+1}^i+p_{t+1}^i(1-\delta_{GK})) \text{ for } i=1,4,5\,.$$

The results are presented in Figure 5. There are no significant differences between them as Hansen's J-statistic supports statistically. Then, we can conclude that private capital and the public capital goods of groups 1, 4 and 5 are efficiently provided.

To consider whether the public capital goods of groups 2 and 3 are too small or too large compared with the efficient level, we calculate the returns of disaggregated public capital goods and compare them with each other. However, we cannot obtain the parameters needed in the calculations since we cannot estimate the capital output elasticities for these public capital goods by GMM. Then, we estimate an aggregate production function. Gramlich (1994) criticized such an approach in the sense that it tended to overestimate the productivities of public capital goods. However, in comparing the returns of disaggregated public capital goods with each other, they provide some useful information.

We incorporate a trend term into (20):

$$Y_t = Ae^{\alpha_0+\alpha_1 t}PK_t^{\beta}GK_{1t}^{\gamma_1}GK_{2t}^{\gamma_2}GK_{3t}^{\gamma_3}GK_{4t}^{\gamma_4}GK_{5t}^{\gamma_5}L_t^{\phi}, \tag{25}$$

where $\alpha_0 + \alpha_1 t$ denotes a trend term. Taking the natural logarithm of (25), we get

$$\ln Y_t = \ln A + \alpha_0 + \alpha_1 t + \beta \ln PK_t + \sum_{i=1}^{5} \gamma_i \ln GK_t^i + \phi \ln L_t . \tag{26}$$

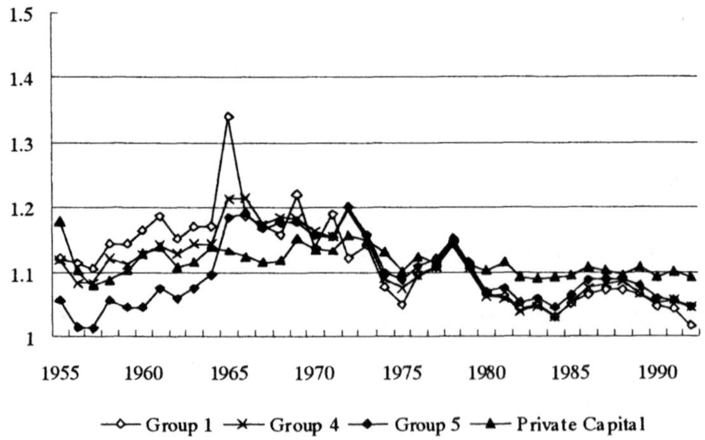

Figure 5. Investment returns (1)

To cope with the serial correlation problem, we estimate the following first difference linear regression model:

$$\Delta \ln Y_t = \alpha_1 + \beta \, \Delta \ln PK_t + \sum_{i=1}^{5} \gamma_i \Delta \ln GK_t^i + \phi \, \Delta \ln L_t \, . \tag{27}$$

The results of OLS may face a serious multicollinearity problem. To cope with it, we use a principal components regression. First, using the eigenvalues and eigenvectors of the correlation matrix of explanatory valuables, we compose principal components. Next, we regress $\Delta \ln Y$ on a constant and some principal components. Substituting the estimated parameters and their variance covariance matrix into the relationship between the components and the explanatory variables, we finally obtain the estimator of the parameters in equation (27) and their variance covariance matrix. The results are reported in Table 4. Cases (ii) and (iii) are the results under the constant-returns-to-scale (CRS) restriction with respect to private inputs and with respect to all inputs respectively. We can say that all types of public capital goods have positive effects on aggregate output to some extent.

Next, with estimates in (i) in Table 4, we calculate the return of each public capital: $(1/p_t^i)(\hat{\gamma}_i Y_{t+1}/GK_{t+1}^i + p_{t+1}^i(1-\delta_{GK}))$ for i=1,...,5. Figure 6 shows the results. The differences among the returns of the public capital goods of groups 1, 4 and 5 have been relatively small. On the other hand, in recent years, the returns for groups 2 and 3 have been diverging upwards from those of the former groups. Provided that the public capital goods of the groups 1, 4 and 5 are efficiently accumulated, the result here indicates that the public capital goods of the groups 2 and 3 are still inadequate compared with the efficient level.

Table 4. Regression results for an aggregate production function

	(i)	(ii)	(iii)
Constant	0.003 (0.225)	-0.002 (-0.207)	0.002 (0.209)
Labor	0.054* (1.983)		
Private capital	0.274** (3.485)	0.108 (1.016)	0.214** (2.421)
Roads, harbors and airports	0.086*** (3.506)	0.109*** (4.811)	0.095*** (4.429)
Railways	0.074** (2.176)	0.122*** (2.834)	0.084*** (2.974)
Postal service, telephone and telegraph	0.109** (2.552)	0.164*** (3.337)	0.131*** (4.753)
Agriculture-related public capitals and fishing ports	0.077*** (3.206)	0.103*** (3.512)	0.078*** (3.657)
Erosions of flood control and conservation of forests	0.041*** (3.249)	0.053*** (4.375)	0.038* (1.770)

Notes: Sample is 1957-1994. The 1, 5 and 10 % critical values are indicated by ***, ** and * respectively.

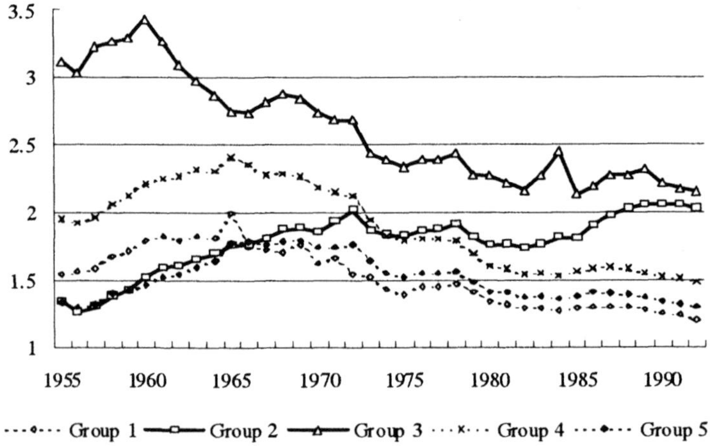

Figure 6. Investment returns (2)

5. CONCLUSION

Our empirical results in this chapter suggest that public capital is sufficiently provided in the aggregate level, but some types of disaggregated public capital goods are still too low compared with the efficient level. Especially, infrastructures for railways, telephone networks, telegraph, and postal services are not being accumulated at efficient levels. Unless the allocation of public works is appropriately revised, it could never stimulate private consumption.

In Japan, an effort is being made to put an additional priority on infrastructure investment to improve the people's lives and the environment in urban area. At the same time, seeking to enhance efficiency and transparency, the efforts to reduce costs and to utilize cost-benefit analysis will be complemented by a new re-assessment system in the near future. These changes are desirable but the speed of structural reform is not so high. A further determined effort is needed to reform public works in a more efficient way.

APPENDIX

The data sources of public capital goods we use are fairly standard in this literature. In Japan, disaggregated data for the 20 types of public capital goods for the sample period FY1953-1993 at prices in CY1990 are available from "Social Capital in Japan" (Economic Planning Agency, 1998). These data are calculated by employing PI method (Perpetual Inventory Method) or BY method (Benchmark Year Method). The original flow data for the 20 types of public investment are defined and calculated in the same way as public fixed capital formation is in the SNA, "Annual Report on National Accounts" (Economic Planning Agency). We use gross domestic product and private final consumption expenditure for the sample period FY1955-1993 at market prices in CY1990 from "Annual Report on National Accounts". Therefore, disaggregated public capital goods data in "Social Capital in Japan" are suitable for our empirical investigations. These 20 types of public capital goods can be classified into two large groups, public capital goods for the production infrastructure and the ones for the living environment.

We pick up the 13 kinds of public capital goods that belong to the former group and sum them up to the following five components:

Group 1: Roads, harbors and airports
(consists of 3 types of public capital goods)

Group 2: Railways
(consists of 3 types of public capital goods)

Group 3: Postal service, telephone and telegraph
(consists of 2 types of public capital goods)
Group 4: Agriculture-related public capitals and fishing ports
(consists of 2 types of public capital goods)
Group 5: Measures for flood control and conservation of forests
(consists of 3 types of public capital goods).

As for private capital goods, we use the gross capital stock data of all enterprises in "Gross Capital Stock of Private Enterprises" (Economic Planning Agency) times operating ratio in "Statistics on Japanese Industries" (Ministry of International Trade and Industry). It must be noted that some public companies were privatized in the 1980s. Nippon Telegraph and Telephone Public Corporation and Japan National Railways (JNR) were privatized in 1985 and in 1987 respectively. They were newly named as Nippon Telegraph and Telephone Company (NTT) and Japan Railways (JR) respectively. The capital stock data of JR and NTT are included in gross capital stock data of all enterprises in "Gross Capital Stock of Private Enterprises". In this paper, they are derived from the private capital stock data and added to Group2 and Group3 respectively.

As for the prices of aggregate output and private sector investment goods, we use deflators of GDP and private sectors gross domestic fixed capital formation for plant and equipment in the "Annual Report on National Accounts" respectively. We can use the deflators of investment goods of 20 types of public sectors, NTT and JR from "Social Capital in Japan". Weighting them with the real values of the investment goods included in that group, we calculate each price of public investmentgoods for the 5 groups.

In estimating the efficiency conditions of public capital, we use per capita consumption data divided by the total population in "Monthly Report on Current Population Estimates" (Management and Coordination Agency).

As for labor supply, we use employed labor force in "Labor Force Survey" (Management and Coordination Agency) times total hours worked indices in manufacturing in "Final Report of Monthly Labor Survey" (the Ministry of Labor).

REFERENCES

Arrow, K. J and M. Kurtz, 1970, *Public Investment, the Rate of Return, and Optimal Fiscal Policy*, Johns Hopkins University Press.

Aschauer, D. A., 1989, Is public expenditure productive? *Journal of Monetary Economics* 23, 177-200.

Asako, K., A. Tsuneki, S. Fukuda, H. Teruyama, T. Tsukamoto and M. Sugiyama, 1994, Productivity of government capital and welfare evaluation of government investment policy, *Economic Analysis* 135, Economic Planning Agency of Japan (in Japanese).

Batina, R. G., 1999, On the long run effects of public capital and disaggregated public capital on aggregate output, *International Tax and Public Finance* 5, 263-281.

Cochrane, J. H., 1991, Production-based asset pricing and the link between stock returns and economic fluctuations, *Journal of Finance* 46, 207-234.

Doi, T., 1998, Panel analysis of public capital in Japan, *Kokumin Keizai* 161, 27-52 (in Japanese).

Gramlich, E. M., 1994, Infrastructure investment: A Review Essay, *Journal of Economic Literature* 32, 1176-1196.

Hansen, L. P., 1982, Large sample properties of generalized method of moments estimations, *Econometrica* 50, 1029-1054.

Hansen, L. P. and K. J. Singleton, 1982, Generalized instrumental variables estimation of nonlinear rational expectations models, *Econometrica* 50, 1269-1286.

Ihori, T., 1987, The size of government spending and the private sector's evaluation, *Journal of Japanese and International Economies* 2, 82-96.

Ihori, T. and H. Kondo, 1998, Public Investment and private consumption: Government deficits and multiplier, *Financial Review* 47, 106-133 (in Japanese).

Ihori, T. and H. Kondo, 2001, Efficiency of disaggregate public capital provision in Japan." *Public Finance and Management* 1, 161-182.

Iwamoto, Y., 1990, An evaluation of public investment policy in postwar Japan, *Economic Review* 41, 250-261 (in Japanese).

Kitasaka, S., 1999, Some tests of the efficiency of public capital provision: Euler equation approach, *JCER Economic Journal* 39, 76-96 (in Japanese).

Kondo, H. and T. Ihori, 1999, The dynamic effects of public investment on private consumption and the welfare implication, *JCER Economic Journal* 39, 55-75 (in Japanese).

Mitsui, K. and K. Ohta, 1995, *Productivity of Public Capital and Public Finance*, Nihon Hyoron Sha (in Japanese).

Otto, G. D. and G. M. Voss, 1998, Is public capital provision efficient? *Journal of Monetary Economics* 42, 47-66.

Yoshino, N. and H. Nakano, 1996, Interregional distribution and productivity effect of public investment, *Financial Review* 41, 16-26 (in Japanese).

Chapter 7

Fiscal Reconstruction

1. INTRODUCTION

We have shown that Barro's neutrality does not hold perfectly in Japan (chapter 2) and there exists a serious concern with the sustainability of fiscal policy in the 1990s (chapter 4). Hence, it is important to reduce government deficits in the long run.

The Japanese government among many governments has been attempting to return to a balanced budget by raising taxes and/or reducing public spending. However, since most transfer payments and public works, which constitute a large part of government expenditures, are actually controlled by interest groups, such attempts often fail. After introducing and raising a consumption tax, Japan's government deficit has grown rapidly, mainly due to increases in transfer payments and public works

Alesina and Drazen (1991) presented a simple model of delayed stabilization due to a war of attrition among various interest groups and derived the expected time of stabilization as a function of characteristics of those groups. Instead of the war of attrition model, Ihori and Itaya (1998) have developed a dynamic game among various interest groups which would accept voluntarily increases in their net tax burden (or abandon some group specific privileges) in order to gain the benefits resulting from a reduction in government debts. Recently, Becker and Mulligan (1998) showed that a "more efficient" tax system such as raising consumption taxes brings larger governments. Velasco (1997) investigated the endogenous path of government debt in the non-cooperative and cooperative dynamic game models and showed that the cooperative equilibrium tends to be violated when the level of debt is low. Based on Velasco (1997), we investigate why fiscal reconstruction attempts would not be successful.

2. THE MODEL

Based on Velasco (1997), in Ihori, Doi and Kondo (2001), we develop an analytical framework which explores the impact of raising taxes on fiscal reconstruction.

Suppose that the economy is divided into n regions and indexed by $i=1,2,\ldots,n$. Regional governments are regarded as interest groups, seeking funds for public works from the central government. For simplicity, we assume that each region is endowed with a unit of population.

The representative individual in each region solves the following optimization problem:

$$\text{MAX} \quad U=\sum_{t=0}^{\infty}\left(\frac{1}{1+\rho}\right)^{t}\ln(C_t^i*), \tag{1}$$

$$\text{s.t.} \quad A_{t+1}^i=(1+r)A_t^i+y-T-C_t^i, \quad \lim_{t\to\infty}\left(\frac{1}{1+r}\right)^{t}A_t^i=0, \tag{2}$$

given A_0^i .

In the objective function (1), ρ is the discount rate, and C_t^i* denotes the level of "effective" consumption in region i in period t, which is taken to the same function as in chapter 6:

$$C_t^i*=C_t^i+\mu(G_{t-1}^i), \quad \mu'>0,\ \mu''<0, \tag{3}$$

where C_t^i and $G_{t-1}{}^i$ denote private consumption and public investment in region i in period t. In the budget constraint (2), A_t^i, r, y and T are assets, interest rate, labor income and lump-sum taxes per capita in region i respectively. The labor income y and the lump-sum tax T are equal among regions and constant over time. For simplicity, we assume that the interest rate r is equal to the discount rate ρ. In this case, keeping the level of effective consumption C_t^i* constant over time is optimal:

$$C^i*=rA_t^i+y-T+\left(\frac{r}{1+r}\right)\sum_{t=0}^{\infty}\left(\frac{1}{1+r}\right)^{t}\mu(G_{t-1}^i). \tag{4}$$

The central government levying tax, issuing debt and allocating public investment among regions faces the following budget constraint:

$$B_{t+1} = (1+r)B_t + \sum_{i=1}^{n} G_t^i - nT \;,\; \lim_{t\to\infty}\left(\frac{1}{1+r}\right)^t B_t = 0, \tag{5}$$

where B_t is the (start-of-period) government debt

The level of the effective consumption C_t^{i*} and the economic welfare depend on the initial net asset A_t^i, the labor income y, the levied tax T, and the sequence of the public investment $\{G_t^i\}_{t=0}^{\infty}$ $(i=1,2,\ldots,n)$. The sequence of public investment must satisfy the budget constraint (5). Public investment per region should be equal to the levied tax T minus the reimbursement of the government debt on average. However, each region may do a larger level of public investment by imposing the additional burden on the other regions. Thus, the crucial point is how the sequence of public investment $\{G_t^i\}_{t=0}^{\infty}$ $(i=1,2,\ldots,n)$ is determined in such situations[1].

The efficient size of public investment G^* that maximizes the joint welfare of all regions is given by

$$1+\rho = \mu'(G^*). \tag{6}$$

However, the efficient size of public investment G^* is not necessarily attained due to the lump-sum tax level T that is not necessarily set to attain it, and the following policy making process. Each region determines the sequence $\{G_t^i\}_{t=0}^{\infty}$ that maximizes (4) for given T, claims it from the central government and brings it to his region. From now on, we assume three constraints on the region's optimization problem. First, no region can claim the public investment that exceeds the optimal level G^*. Second, each region must preserve the intertemporal budget constraint of the central government, namely the transversality condition. Third, the lump-sum tax T is pre-determined by the central government, and hence is taken as given by regions. Under these assumptions we can describe the optimization problem that the regions face as the following:

$$\text{MAX} \quad \sum_{t=0}^{\infty}\left(\frac{1}{1+r}\right)^t \mu(G_t^i)$$

[1] The change in the lump-sum tax never affects the level of consumption as long as the sequence of the public investment $\{G_t^i\}_{t=0}^{\infty}$ is not changed (see chapter 2). However, if a change in the lump-sum tax affects the sequence of the public investment, it could affect the level of the effective consumption and the economic welfare.

s.t. (5), $G_t \leq G^*$,

given B_0.

We analyze the equilibrium dynamic process in the following two cases. First, all regions act in a coordinated fashion to maximize joint welfare. In this case all interest groups agree with fiscal reconstruction. Furthermore, the central government can attain the first best level of public investment by setting the constant lump-sum tax T in the proper level. Second, all region behave non-cooperatively. In this case fiscal reconstruction is not effectively conducted by the central government.

In the first cooperative case, the equilibrium level of public investment per region is given as:

$$G = MIN\left[-r\frac{B_t}{n} + T, G^*\right]. \tag{7}$$

Since the rate of time preference is equal to the rate of interest and the marginal benefit of public capital decreases with G, it is desirable to keep public investment as well as private consumption constant over time as the cooperative solution[2].

From (5) and (7), we can see how an unexpected permanent increase in the lump-sum tax levied by the central government affects public investment per region and private consumption:

$$\frac{dG}{dT} = 1. \tag{8}$$

$$\frac{dB_t}{dT} = 0, \quad t = 1,2,\cdots. \tag{9}$$

That is, the increase in public investment is just equal to the increase in the central government's permanent tax revenue, not affecting the dynamics of public debt.

Next, let us turn to the case of a non-cooperative dynamic game among regions. Since maximization problem is identical for all regions, optimal policy for each region should be identical too. The optimal policy is the function of state variable B_t, but it is bounded by G^*:

$$G_t = MIN[h(B_t), G^*]. \tag{10}$$

[2] The transversality condition in (5) will be violated (negatively) if the lump-sum tax exceeds G^*+rB_t/n. We assume that the central government never levies such a heavy tax.

Hence, each region faces the following budget constraint obtained by substituting (10) into (5):

$$G_t = B_{t+1} - (1+r)B_t - (n-1)h(B_t) + nT \quad \text{if} \quad h(B_t) \leq G^*,$$
$$G_t = B_{t+1} - (1+r)B_t - (n-1)G^* + nT \quad \text{if} \quad h(B_t) \geq G^*. \tag{11}$$

As shown in Appendix, if the following condition is not satisfied, the level of the public investmentper region is G^*;

$$B_t \geq \frac{nT}{r} + \frac{G^*}{\phi(1+r)}. \tag{12}$$

Then, from (11) the debt evolves as the following:

$$B_{t+1} = (1+r)B_t + n(G^* - T). \tag{13}$$

If condition (12) is satisfied, the level of the public investment per region is given as $h(B_t)$. We have then

$$B_{t+1} = (1+r)(1+n\phi)B_t + nT\left\{\frac{1-(1+r)(1+n\phi)}{r}\right\}, \tag{14}$$

$$0 < \frac{G_{\tau+1}}{G_\tau} = [1+(n-1)\phi]^{/1-\alpha} < 1. \tag{15}$$

The steady state government bondis given by

$$B = \frac{nT}{r}. \tag{16}$$

Figure 1 shows the dynamic behavior of the government debt Line *BB* and *B'B'* correspond to (13) and (14) respectively. The public investment falls as the government debt rises and in the limit they converge to zero and a finite level respectively. Intuition is as follows. When public debt is high, each regional government believes that other regional governments would reduce public investment (h'<0), reducing the effective rate of interest of financing public debt, $(1+r)+(n-1)h'$. This stimulates the free-riding behavior. Namely, since the effective rate of interest declines with public debt, each regional government desires a high level of public investment at the early stage of the game. Each region perceives that other regions will pay some parts of the government debt redemption by reducing their public investment in the future.

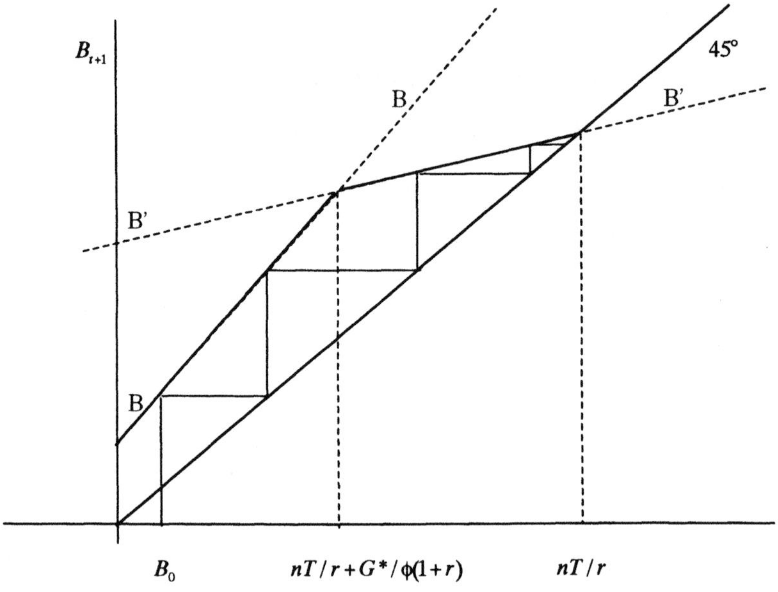

Figure1. Dynamics of government debt

We now consider how an unexpected permanent increase in lump-sum tax affects the dynamic behavior of public investment per region and government debt. The public investment per region in each period from now on changes by

$$\frac{dG_t}{dT} = -\{(1+r)(1+n\phi)\}^t \left\{\frac{\phi(1+r)n}{r}\right\}, \tag{17}$$

compared with its original level. The steady state government debt changes by

$$\frac{dB}{dT} = \frac{n}{r}. \tag{18}$$

Note that (17) is positive since ϕ is negative. Therefore, both public investment and steady state government debt rise as the lump-sum tax rises. The dynamics are shown in Figure 2. Under the situation of the non-cooperative dynamic game, the permanent increase in the lump-sum tax stimulates public investment only in the short run, and it causes an expansion of the government debt

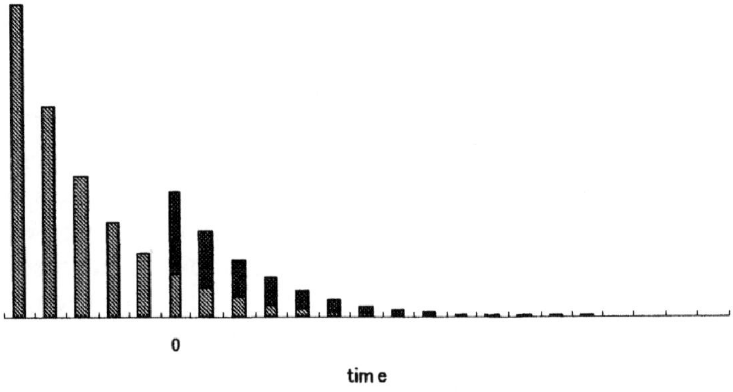

Public investment

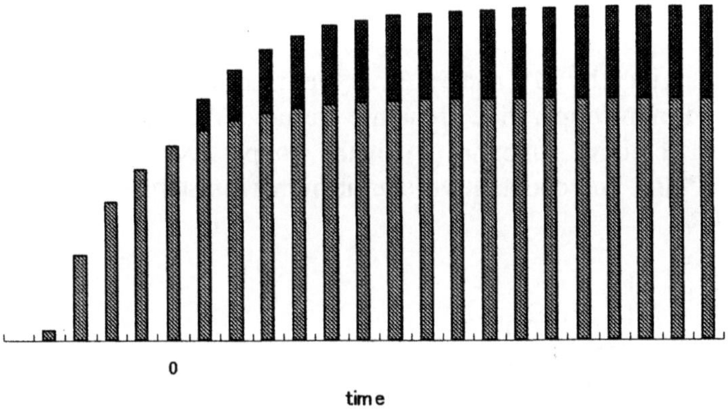

Public debt

Figure2. Dynamics of public investment and public debt

To apply this model to the fiscal reconstruction process, some applicable implications are obtained. Namely, the impact of a tax increase on public debt can tell whether fiscal reconstruction may be regarded as a cooperative one or not. According to (8) and (9), in the case where all interest groups act in a coordinated fashion, an increase in tax revenues leads to an increase in public investment or privileges by the same amount, and not to a change in the public debt. On the other hand, according to (17) and (18) (see Figure 2), in the case where each interest group acts non-cooperatively, an increase in revenues leads to an increase in the public debt as well as an increase in public investment. By investigating whether (9) or (18) is held in the real economy, we may explore the dynamic nature of the fiscal reconstruction process.

Before doing some empirical studies, it would be useful to investigate how the central government could induce regions to agree with a switch from the non-cooperative dynamic game equilibrium to the cooperative one. Analytically this problem may be considered as whether the cooperative equilibrium is stable or not. We examine it by introducing trigger strategies.

Suppose in period 0 the cooperative equilibrium is attained. If the cooperative equilibrium has been maintained in all t-1 preceding periods, regions cooperate in the period t too; otherwise, they switch to the non-cooperative dynamic gameequilibrium.

A region that defects from the cooperation solves

$$W^d(B_0) = MAX \ \mu(G_0^i) + \left(\frac{1}{1+r}\right)W(B_1) \tag{19}$$

$$\text{s.t.} \quad B_1 = (1+r)B_0 + G_0^i + (n-1)G_0 - nT\,,\ G_t \le G^*,$$

where G_0 is given by (7), and $W(B_t)$ is the maximized objective function in the case of non-cooperative dynamic game. We define $W^*(B_0)$ as the maximized objective function (7) in the cooperative situation. If $W^d(B_0)$ exceeds $W^*(B_0)$, the cooperative equilibrium is unstable at the government debt level B_0.

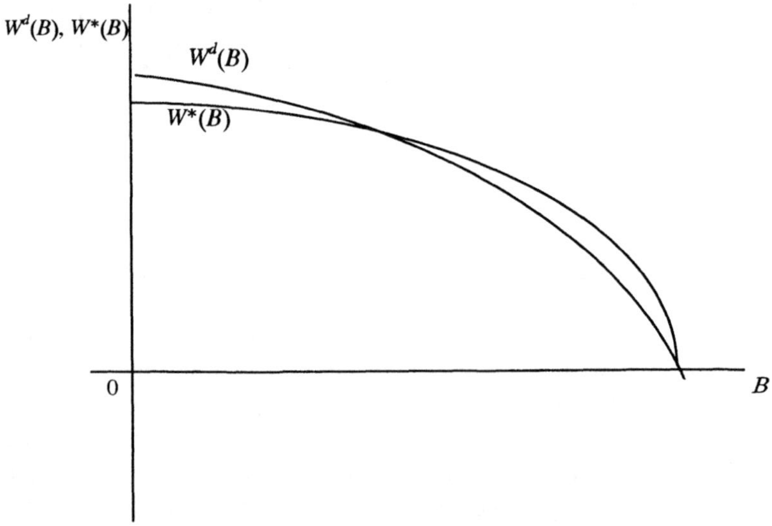

Figure3. Economic welfare

Figure 3 shows the possibility of this defection. Under the non-cooperative dynamic game, the later the consensus of fiscal reconstruction is attained, the more difficult to confirm it. This is a different result from Velasco (1997). Intuition is as follows. A switch from the cooperative dynamic game to the non-cooperative dynamic game produces a gain in the early stage and a loss in the late stage. When public debt is high, the stationary level of public spending becomes low and hence the gain in the early stage would outweigh the loss in the late stage of the game.

3. ESTIMATION

We analyze the General Account (excluding grants of local allocation tax) in FY 1955-1997. In the General Account, expenditures by purpose are divided into the following categories; national agencies, local government finance, national defense, disposition of external affairs, national land conservation and development (public works), industrial development, education and culture, social security, pensions, government bonds and other. Based on the above model, we can divide these variables as follows. The first group is expenditures for provision of pure public goods, including national agencies, national defense, disposition of external affairs, and education and culture, denoted by Z. The second is interest payment, equal to government bonds minus bond redemption, denoted by rB. The last one is public investment and privileges to regions, including the remaining expenditures (excluding grantsof local allocation tax), denoted by $\sum_{i=1}^{n} G_t^i$.

On the revenue side, we divide the total revenue into tax and other revenues (T) and net issue of debt (equal to public debt minus bond redemption: $\Delta B \equiv B_t - B_{t-1}$), excluding revenues for grants of local allocation tax. We use these variables deflated by the GDP deflator.

We can apply literature on the revenue-expenditure nexus to our investigation. There exist many previous studies on the relationship between revenues and expenditures in the U.S.; e.g. von Fustenberg, Green and Jeong (1985, 1986), Manage and Marlow (1986), Holtz-Eakin, Newey and Rosen (1989), and Owoye (1995).

In previous works, the Granger causality tests using the conventional VAR analysis and ECMs have been used. One of these shortcomings is the tests cannot be implemented when the orders of integration of revenues and expenditures are different, or when either order of integration is more than two. To avoid it, we employ the method of Toda and Yamamoto (1995)[3].

[3] An example that employs this method on the revenue-expenditure nexus is Doi (1998).

An advantage of this method is that we can implement the Granger causality tests when the order of integration of revenues is not equal to that of expenditures and when either order of integration is more than two. The method is as follows.

We consider the following VAR of an N-vector time series $\{\mathbf{X}_t\}_{t=-\kappa+1}^{\infty}$ ($\kappa \geq 1$):

$$\mathbf{X}_t = \mathbf{b}_0 + \mathbf{b}_1\mathbf{t} + \Phi_1\mathbf{X}_{t-1} + \cdots + \Phi_\kappa\mathbf{X}_{t-\kappa} + \cdots + \Phi_l\mathbf{X}_{t-l} + \boldsymbol{\varepsilon}_t, \tag{20}$$

where $\mathbf{X}_t \equiv \begin{bmatrix} X_{1t} \\ X_{2t} \\ \vdots \\ X_{nt} \end{bmatrix}$, $\Phi_i \equiv \begin{bmatrix} \varphi^i_{11} & \varphi^i_{12} & \cdots & \varphi^i_{1N} \\ \varphi^i_{21} & \varphi^i_{22} & & \\ \vdots & & \ddots & \vdots \\ \varphi^i_{N1} & & \cdots & \varphi^i_{NN} \end{bmatrix}$,

Φ_i ($i = 1,2, \ldots, \kappa, \ldots, l$) denotes an N×N matrix of coefficients, **t** denotes a vector of a time trend, and $\boldsymbol{\varepsilon}_t$ denotes an N-vector of the innovation. We assume that the order of integration of $\mathbf{X}_t$ is at most d_{max} around a linear trend. d_{max} denotes the maximal order of integration of variables in $\mathbf{X}_t$.

First, we select the lag length in (20). According to Toda and Yamamoto (1995), under the following null hypothesis:

$$H'_0: \Phi_{m+1} = \ldots = \Phi_l = \mathbf{0}, \qquad \text{where } \kappa \leq m \leq l-1$$

the usual Wald statistic obtained from the OLS estimators of coefficients in (20), has an asymptotic χ^2 distribution with $N^2(l-m)$ degrees of freedom if $m \geq d_{max}$. After this test, we select the lag length as the null hypothesis can be rejected. λ denotes the selected lag length.

For implementing the Granger causality tests, we estimate the following VAR:

$$\mathbf{X}_t = \mathbf{b}_0 + \mathbf{b}_1\mathbf{t} + \Phi_1\mathbf{X}_{t-1} + \cdots + \Phi_\kappa\mathbf{X}_{t-\kappa} + \cdots + \Phi_\lambda\mathbf{X}_{t-\lambda} + \boldsymbol{\varepsilon}_t, \tag{21}$$

In this regression, the *i*-th variable, X_{it}, does not Granger-cause the *j*-th variable, X_{jt}, if we cannot reject the following null hypothesis:

$$H_0: \varphi^1_{ji} = \ldots = \varphi^\lambda_{ji} = 0.$$

Toda and Yamamoto (1995) proved that under the above null hypothesis, the usual Wald statistic obtained from the OLS estimators of coefficients in (21), has an asymptotic χ^2 distribution with λ degrees of freedom if $\lambda \geq \kappa + d_{max}$. Note that the conditions, $\lambda \geq \kappa + d_{max}$ and $\kappa \geq 1$, must be satisfied.

We analyze a VAR model with the following five endogenous variables: $\frac{Z}{Y}$, $\frac{\sum_{i=1}^{n} G_t^i}{Y}$, $\frac{T}{Y}$, and $\frac{\Delta B}{Y}$ (or $\frac{B}{Y}$), where Y denotes GDP.

Before the Granger causality tests, we implement the unit root tests. We employ the augmented Dickey-Fuller tests because the number of observation of these variables is not large enough to implement the Phillips-Perron tests. We use the criteria advocated by Pantula, Gonzalez-Farias and Fuller (1994), and based on the principle of parsimony in deciding the lag length.

We found the order of integration of each variable by the augmented Dickey-Fuller tests. We set the 5% significance level in testing the null hypothesis that the variable has a unit root. The order of integration of each variable is identified by the tests. From these results, we set d_{max}=2 as the larger of the order of integration of the five variables; $\frac{Z}{Y}$, $\frac{\sum_{i=1}^{n} G_t^i}{Y}$, $\frac{T}{Y}$, and $\frac{\Delta B}{Y}$ (or $\frac{B}{Y}$).

In the next step, we select the lag length of VAR. As mentioned above, we decide the lag length, λ, using the Wald statistic. We note that the conditions, $\lambda \geq \kappa + d_{max}$ and $\kappa \geq 1$, must be satisfied. As a result, we set $\lambda = 3$.

We estimate the VAR equations (21), with a lag length equal to 3. The results are reported in Table 1. We then implement the Granger causality tests based on the Wald statistics from the OLS estimators. The Wald statistics are reported in Table 2. Figure 4 summarizes the results of the Granger causality tests.

According to the Granger causality tests, we confirm that the causality from $\frac{T}{Y}$ to $\frac{\sum_{i=1}^{n} G_t^i}{Y}$ as well as from $\frac{T}{Y}$ to $\frac{\Delta B}{Y}$ (or $\frac{B}{Y}$) is strong. It suggests that an increase in the tax revenues leads to an increase in privileges as well as a decrease in the net issuance of public debt in the Japanese fiscal reconstruction, which is consistent with the analytical result of non-cooperative dynamic game in the previous section. Also, an increase in taxes leads to an increase in the level of public debt outstanding, which is consistent with the result of non-cooperative dynamic game too. In other words, the Japanese government was not strong enough to persuade interest groups to cooperate with fiscal reconstruction in the above sample period. We could not exclude freeriding behavior of interesting groups.

Table1. Estimation of the VAR

	Dependent variable:				Dependent variable:			
	$(G/Y)_t$	$(T/Y)_t$	$(Z/Y)_t$	$(B/Y)_t$	$(G/Y)_t$	$(T/Y)_t$	$(Z/Y)_t$	$(\Delta B/Y)_t$
intercept	0.006	0.075	0.002	-0.062	0.033	0.056	-0.008	-0.030
	(0.808)	(4.030)	(0.129)	(-1.852)	(2.587)	(3.484)	(-1.553)	(-1.719)
Timetrend	0.366	-0.912	0.526	1.706	-0.029	-0.094	0.003	0.065
$X10^3$	(3.471)	(-3.517)	(2.262)	(3.668)	(-0.326)	(-0.830)	(0.101)	(0.524)
$(G/Y)_{t-1}$	-0.153	0.216	0.840	-1.676	21.847	12.274	6.325	15.764
	(-1.463)	(0.840)	(3.642)	(-3.629)	(1.980)	(0.886)	(1.518)	(1.038)
$(G/Y)_{t-2}$	-0.130	0.525	0.144	1.610	24.844	-13.399	4.822	43.078
	(-0.864)	(1.421)	(0.435)	(2.433)	(2.604)	(-1.119)	(1.339)	(3.283)
$(G/Y)_{t-3}$	0.201	-0.105	0.160	-0.551	-6.491	-4.301	-3.471	-5.485
	(1.989)	(-0.423)	(0.718)	(-1.234)	(-0.645)	(-0.341)	(-0.914)	(-0.396)
$(T/Y)_{t-1}$	0.169	0.172	0.062	1.527	-21.138	-11.873	-6.179	-15.302
	(2.760)	(0.778)	(0.312)	(3.857)	(-1.907)	(-0.853)	(-1.477)	(-1.004)
$(T/Y)_{t-2}$	0.100	-0.593	-0.079	-0.607	-24.842	13.491	-4.736	-43.092
	(0.945)	(-2.277)	(-0.339)	(-1.300)	(-2.602)	(1.125)	(-1.314)	(-3.281)
$(T/Y)_{t-3}$	-0.064	-0.142	-0.156	0.423	6.258	3.760	3.482	5.807
	(-1.088)	(-0.979)	(-1.203)	(1.634)	(0.626)	(0.299)	(0.922)	(0.422)
$(Z/Y)_{t-1}$	0.314	0.667	-0.063	-1.313	21.936	12.821	6.972	15.918
	(1.558)	(1.345)	(-0.141)	(-1.476)	(1.954)	(0.909)	(1.645)	(1.030)
$(Z/Y)_{t-2}$	-0.317	1.180	0.452	-1.621	24.296	-14.040	4.551	42.941
	(-1.447)	(2.191)	(0.937)	(-1.678)	(2.492)	(-1.147)	(1.236)	(3.201)
$(Z/Y)_{t-2}$	-0.067	-0.768	-0.444	1.773	-6.611	-3.260	-3.264	-6.447
	(-0.500)	(-2.344)	(-1.513)	(3.015)	(-0.667)	(-0.262)	(-0.872)	(-0.472)
$(B/Y)_{t-1}$	0.162	-0.086	0.137	2.708				
	(2.540)	(-0.551)	(0.977)	(9.650)				
$(B/Y)_{t-2}$	-0.116	-0.477	-0.341	-1.905				
	(-0.939)	(-1.573)	(-1.254)	(-3.503)				
$(B/Y)_{t-3}$	-0.081	0.643	0.153	0.070				
	(-0.963)	(3.122)	(0.832)	(0.189)				
$(\Delta B/Y)_{t-1}$					-20.939	-12.348	-6.174	-14.623
					(-1.894)	(-0.890)	(-1.479)	(-0.961)
$(\Delta B/Y)_{t-2}$					-24.952	13.522	-4.761	-43.257
					(-2.620)	(1.131)	(-1.324)	(-3.302)
$(\Delta B/Y)_{t-3}$					6.435	4.110	3.489	5.643
					(0.643)	(0.327)	(0.924)	(0.410)
	log of likelihood function 722.274				log of likelihood function 908.027			
std. error	0.001	0.003	0.003	0.006	0.003	0.004	0.001	0.004
Adj. R^2	0.806	0.873	0.978	0.999	0.931	0.819	0.989	0.941
D.W.	2.190	2.401	2.032	1.877	2.075	2.113	2.061	2.029

Note:
a. sample: 1955-1997.
b. The above parentheses indicate the t-values.

Table2. Granger causality tests; Wald statistics

Dependent Variable	Independent variables			
	ΣG/Y	T/Y	Z/Y	B/Y
ΣG/Y	--	6.626 (0.036)	7.334 (0.026)	10.801 (0.005)
T/Y	9.922 (0.007)	--	6.927 (0.031)	13.479 (0.001)
Z/Y	0.918 (0.632)	0.156 (0.925)	--	1.585 (0.453)
B/Y	7.698 (0.021)	14.890 (0.001)	13.216 (0.001)	--

Dependent Variable	Independent variables			
	ΣG/Y	T/Y	Z/Y	B/Y
ΣG/Y	--	11.580 (0.003)	11.631 (0.003)	11.597 (0.003)
T/Y	1.861 (0.394)	--	1.886 (0.390)	1.884 (0.390)
Z/Y	4.534 (0.104)	4.363 (0.113)	--	4.391 (0.111)
B/Y	12.634 (0.002)	12.063 (0.002)	12.490 (0.002)	--

Note:

a. Sample: 1955-1997.

b. The above parentheses indicate the p-values of the hypothesis: The independent variable does not Granger-cause the dependent variable.

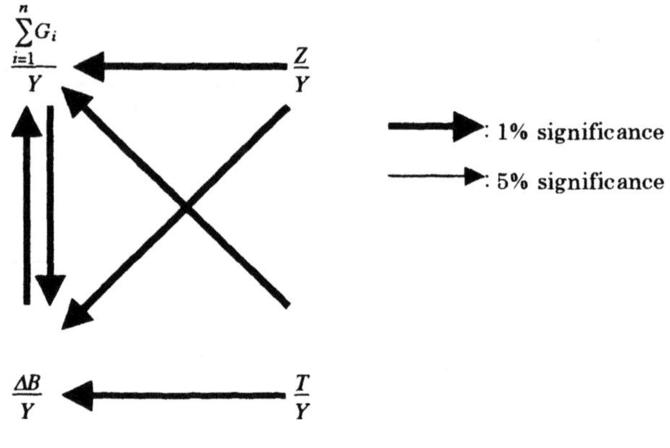

Figure4. Granger causality tests

4. CONCLUSION

The most important policy's lesson from these analyses is that if the program of fiscal reconstruction is too flexible in the sense that it allows each interest group to reconsider the predetermined policies such as tax increases or subsidy cuts at each point in time when the outcome of fiscal reconstruction is revealed, it is highly likely that fiscal reconstruction ends in failure. Allowing such a possibility would strengthen the incentive of each group to free ride. In order to realize successful fiscal reconstruction, therefore, we have to stick to the long-term program for fiscal reconstruction that has been agreed at the beginning of planning period. In practice, one of the most effective means is to enact legislation for fiscal reconstruction, which does not permit much room for reconsidering or revising the fiscal reconstruction plan. In the real economy both the Gramm-Rudman-Hollings Act in the United States and the Fiscal Structural Reform Act in Japan have a weakness in that they allow considerable room for reconsidering the fiscal reform.

APPENDIX

We investigate the characteristics of the function $h(B_t)$. Here we specify the function μ as

$$\mu(G) = G^{\alpha} \quad , 0 < \alpha < 1. \tag{A1}$$

Substituting (11) and (A1) into (13) and differentiating it with respect to $\{B_t\}_{t=1}^{\infty}$, we obtain the following first order condition:

$$G_{t+1} = G_t \left[1 + \frac{n-1}{1+r} h'(B_{t+1}) \right]^{1/1-\alpha} . \tag{A2}$$

Since the policy function of this region is also given as (10), (11) and (A2) can be rewritten as

$$B_{t+1} = (1+r)B_t + nh(B_t) - nT , \tag{11'}$$

$$h(B_{t+1}) = h(B_t) \left[1 + \frac{n-1}{1+r} h'(B_{t+1}) \right]^{1/1-\alpha} . \tag{A2'}$$

Substituting (11)' into (A2)', we obtain:

$$h((1+r)B + nh(B) - nT) = h(B) \left[1 + \frac{n-1}{1+r} h'((1+r)B + nh(B) - nT) \right]^{1/1-\alpha} . \tag{A3}$$

We guess that the function $h(B_t)$ takes the following liner form:

$$h(B_t) = \phi(1+r)B_t + \theta . \tag{A4}$$

Substituting (A4) into (A3), we obtain the conditions that the parameters ϕ, θ must satisfy:

$$(1+r)(1+n\phi) = \{1 + (n-1)\phi\}^{1/1-\alpha} , \tag{A5}$$

$$\{1 + \phi(1+r)n\}\theta = \theta\{1 + (n-1)\phi\}^{1/1-\alpha} + \phi(1+r)nT . \tag{A6}$$

The parameter ϕ satisfies

$$-1/(n-1) < \phi < 0 . \tag{A7}$$

From (A5) and (A6), the parameter θ is given by

$$\theta = -\frac{\phi(1+r)nT}{r}. \tag{A8}$$

Remember that the function $h(B_t)$ is the optimal reaction function if it is smaller than G^*. From (A4) and (A8), we can see that $h(B_t)$ is the reaction function if

$$B_t \geq \frac{nT}{r} + \frac{G^*}{\phi(1+r)}.$$

If the above condition is satisfied, the level of the public investment per region is given as $h(B_t)$. Using (11)(A2)(A4)(A7) and (A8), we have then (14) and (15).

REFERENCES

Alesina, A. and A. Drazen, 1991, Why is stabilization delayed? *American Economic Review* 81, 1170-1188.

Becker, G.S. and C.B. Mulligan, 1998, Deadweight costs and the size of government, *NBER working paper* #6789.

Doi, T., 1998, Is Japanese local finance really centralized?: From a viewpoint of the revenue-expenditure nexus, *Institute of Social Science Discussion Paper Series* F-76, University of Tokyo.

Holtz-Eakin, D., W. Newey and H. Rosen, 1989, The revenue-expenditure nexus: Evidence from local government data, *International Economic Review* 30, 415-429.

Ihori, T. and J. Itaya, 1998, A dynamic analysis of fiscal reconstruction, *mimeo.*

Ihori, T., T. Doi and H. Kondo, 2001, Japanese fiscal reform: Fiscal reconstruction and fiscal policy, *Japan and the World Economy* 13, 351-370.

Manage, M.L. and N. Marlow, 1986, The causal relation between federal government expenditures and receipts, *Southern Journal of Economics* 52, 617-629.

Owoye, O., 1995, The causal relationship between taxes and expenditures in the G7 countries: Cointegration and error-correction models, *Applied Economic Letters* 2, 19-22.

Pantula, S.G., G. Gonzalez-Farias and W.A. Fuller, 1994, A comparison of unit-root test criteria, *Journal of Business and Economic Statistics* 12, 449-459.

Toda, H.Y. and T. Yamamoto, 1995, Statistical inference in vector autoregressions with possibly integrated processes, *Journal of Econometrics* 66, 225-250.

von Furstenberg, G.M., R.J. Green and J.-H. Jeong, 1985, Have taxes led government expenditures? The United States as a test case, *Journal of Public Policy* 5, 321-348.

von Furstenberg, G.M., R.J. Green and J.-H. Jeong, 1986, Tax and spend, or spend and tax? *Review of Economics and Statistics* 68, 179-188.

Velasco, A., 1997, A model of endogenous fiscal deficits and delayed fiscal reforms, *NBER Working paper* #6336.

Chapter 8

The System and Role of Local Bonds Permits in Japan

1. INTRODUCTION

In the 1990s, local public finance in Japan largely depended on the issue of bonds for revenue, because of a slowdown of economic growth and a decrease in tax revenue.[1] Local bonds cumulatively increased as follows: by the end of FY 2000 they had reached around 180 trillion yen, 35% of GDP, about 1.8 times as large as the total local expenditures (about 100 trillion yen), and about 2.5 times as large as in FY 1990. Local Bonds and other borrowings that will be redeemed by local governments are shown in Figure 1.

In Japan, local governments cannot freely issue local bonds. Japan has a system that local governments must obtain permission from the Minister of Home Affairs (the present Minister of Public Management, Home Affairs, Posts and Telecommunications) in advance when they issue local bonds. Therefore the permission of the central government as well as needs of local governments led to the above increase of local bonds

Under the current intergovernmental system in Japan, the System of Local Bonds Permits is managed as a part of the control tools of the central government. Besides local bonds, rates and sources of local taxes are basically determined by national laws, and the Local Transfer Taxes, the Local Allocation Tax (LAT) , and the National Government Disbursements are distributed to local governments by the central government, especially the (former) Ministry of Home Affairs (MOHA; the present Ministry of Public Management, Home Affairs, Posts and Telecommunications).

[1] In Japan, the word ‘local governments’ implies prefectures and municipalities.

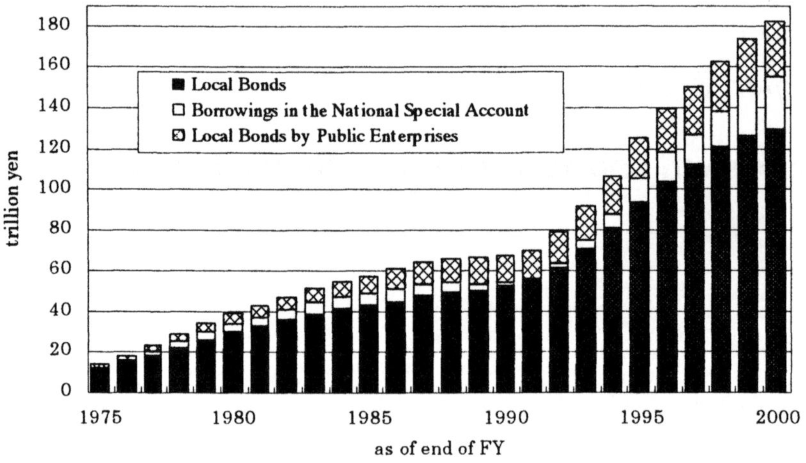

Figure1. Outstandings of local government borrowing

The permission for issuing local bonds includes not only the volume of issuance but also the lenders of the bonds. The lenders mainly consist of the Trust Fund Bureau (TFB) of the Ministry of Finance, the Japan Finance Corporations for Municipal Enterprises (JFM), and private financial institutions. The lenders of local bonds are basically decided not by local governments but by the Minister of Home Affairs. Using econometric analysis we examine how the Minister of Home Affairs decides volumes and lenders of local bondsunder the.

Takayori (1988) and Nakano (2000) are two of the previous studies on the System of Local Bonds Permits. We comprehensively analyze the system for the first time. Under the above situation, we need objective investigations into reasons why the MOHA permits increases in the issuance of local bonds.

The remainder of this paper is organized as follows: We explain the system and management of Local Bonds Permits in Section 2. Section 3 proposes hypotheses to assess explain the system and management based on descriptions of policy makers and economic theories. We empirically examine the hypotheses using data on Japanese prefectural finance and economy in Section 4. Finally, Section 5 concludes our analysis on the system.

2. RELATIONSHIP BETWEEN THE SYSTEM OF LOCAL BONDS PERMITS AND NATIONAL BUDGET[2]

2.1 The system of Local Bonds Permits

The System of Local Bonds Permits requires local governments to obtain permission from the Minister of Home Affairs in advance when they issue local bonds.[3] Thus local governments cannot freely issue local bonds

Article 5 of the Local Finance Law provides the expenditures that may be financed by local bonds. Revenue by local bonds may be spent on (1) expenditures for services which in the future, will create revenue for the repayment of the borrowing, (2) bond redemption by refunding bonds, (3) expenditures for services which local governments are obliged to provide because of extraordinary and unexpected events, and (4) expenditures for services whose effects will persist, and which promote development of regional economy and increase local tax revenue which, in the future, can be spent on repayment of the borrowing. Besides the above expenditures, the minister of home affairs exceptionally permits issuance of bonds for financial reconstruction of local governments, bonds for development in depopulated areas, bonds for retirement allowance payments and so on.

Moreover, the Local Autonomy Law and the Local Finance Law, which are national laws, provide that the following local governments cannot issue local bonds. The local governments, which the ratio of deficits of net balance to the Standard Financial Scale is more than a set level (5% for prefectures and 20% for municipalities), cannot issue local bonds for public works excluding bond for financial reconstruction of local governments.[4] In addition, the following local governments cannot be permitted to issue local

[2] We use names of the ministries and agencies until 2000 in this paper. Also we explain the Japanese fiscal system based on it until 2000 in this paper. We will assess the system for the years 1975-1997. We refer to Shibata (1993) and Naruse and Isozaki (1997) for names in English.

[3] Strictly speaking, prefectures must obtain permission from the Minister of Home Affairs, and municipalities must obtain permission from the Governor of the prefecture. The Minister of Home Affairs guides the prefectural governors in giving permission. Thus, in practice, the Minister of Home Affairs controls the permission.

[4] In Japan, net balance = the total revenue – the total expenditure – expenses brought forward, and the Standard Financial Scale = the Regular Allocation Tax + the Local Transfer Taxes + (the Standard Financial Revenue – the Local Transfer Taxes)×(1 – β). The Standard Financial Scale means general income resources that the local governments obtain in a normal situation; ex. ordinary taxes (stipulated in the Local Tax Law), the Regular Allocation Tax, and the Local Transfer Taxes. β denotes the portion that the local governments can be used freely, and is 20% for prefectures and 25% for municipalities.

bonds: a local government which has arrearages of redemption, whose ratio of tax collection to estimated tax revenue in the year is less than 90%, whose tax rate is less than the standard tax rate provided by the Local Tax Law, and whose average of debt expenditure ratio (used as permission to issue local bonds) of the past three fiscal years is more than 20%.

Under provisions of the above laws, the permission for issuing local bonds to each local government is decided in the following budget process. Before deciding the volume of issuance of local bonds, the Ministry of Finance (MOF) negotiates with other ministries about the National Government Disbursement (specific matching grants) of the budget in the next fiscal year in the national budget process. At the same time, the MOF negotiates with the MOHA about the national and local tax system (rates and sources) in the next fiscal year. Then the MOF (and the MOHA about only estimated revenue from local taxes) drafts the budget of expenditures (except the Grants for Local Allocation Tax) in the General Account (including the National Government Disbursement) and national and local tax revenue. The MOHA estimates the expenditures in the next year of all local governments. After the estimation, the MOF finally negotiates with the MOHA about the LAT and issuance of local bonds. At the same time, the MOF decides volume of issuance of national bonds and borrowing from the Fiscal Investment and Loan (FIL) funds. As shown in Figure 2, the volume of local bonds is affected by that of the LAT and the FIL funds. Doi and Nakazato (1998) and Doi (2000) analyze the decision-making. We examine it in detail in the next section.

2.2 Relationship between the Local Public Finance Program, the Local Bond Program, and the Fiscal Investment and Loan Program[5]

The source of the LAT is a certain percentage of the national taxes in the General Account. The Grants for Local Allocation Tax are transferred from the General Account to the Special Account for Allocation and Transfer Taxes. Then the LAT is allocated from the Special Account to a local government whose tax revenue is relatively smaller. If the source of the LAT is smaller than the shortfall of local revenue estimated by the MOHA (it is always smaller in practice), the MOF and the MOHA supplement the shortfall by the following instruments. At first, the MOF agrees increments of transfer from the General Account to the Special Account for Allocation and Transfer Taxes. As a result, issuance of national bonds in the General

[5] We refer to Zaisei Chosa Kai, "National Budget" (various years) for opinions of the Ministry of Finance, and to the Ministry of Home Affairs, "Local Finance" (various issues) for those of the Ministry of Home Affairs.

Account increases, though the increment of the LAT is not directly financed by national bonds, as shown in Figure 2. In addition, the borrowings in the Special Account for Allocation and Transfer Taxes are used as a source of the LAT. However, the shortfall doesn't disappear.

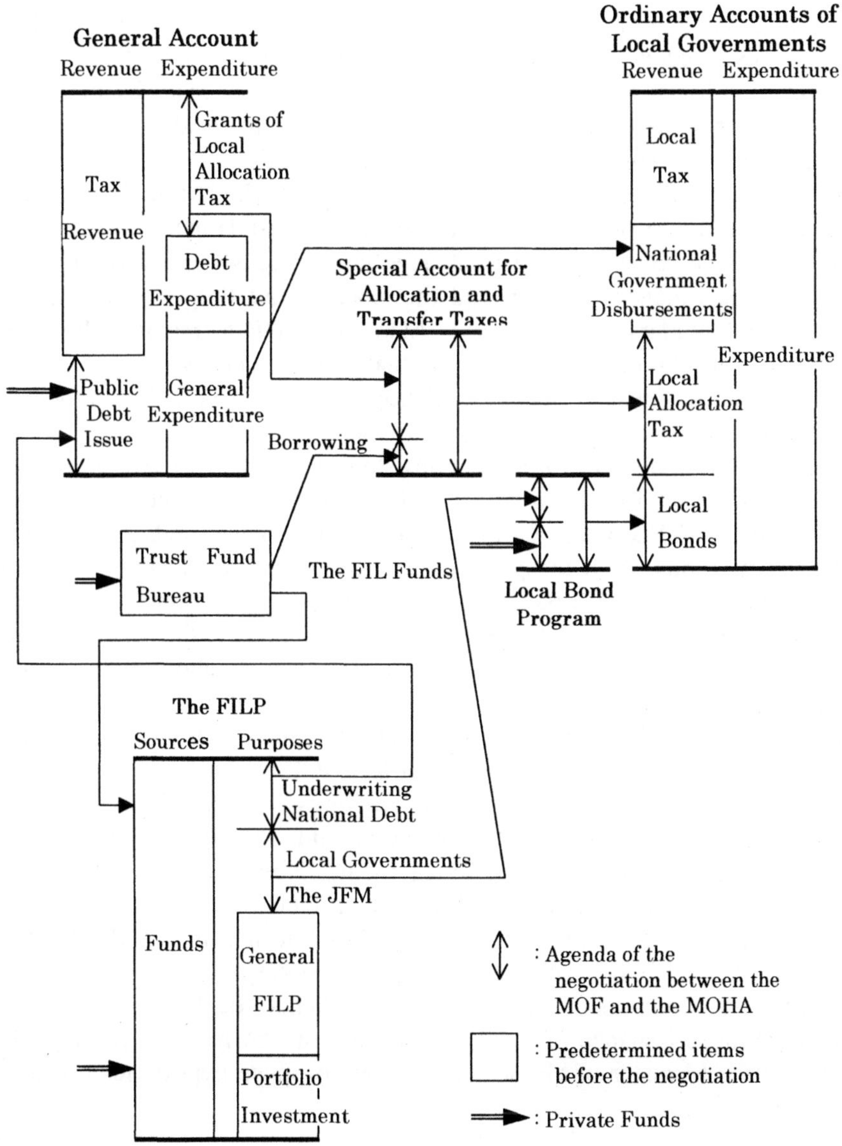

Local Transfer Tax is eliminated from the above figure.

Figure 2. Relationship between the national budget and local public finance

And finally, the MOHA agrees increments of local bonds. Local governments want increments of the LAT, because they can decrease issuance of local bonds and their heavier financial burdens in the future. On the contrary, the MOF want increments of local bonds in the final negotiation, because issuance of national bonds and their heavier financial burdens in the future in the General Account decrease. At the same time, the MOF negotiates with the MOHA about (estimated) lenders of national and local bonds, especially borrowing from the FIL funds. The interest rate of FIL funds is lower than that of private funds. And the maturity of the FIL funds is longer than that of private funds. Therefore local governments as well as the MOF want to borrow from the FIL funds.[6]

Then the MOF formulates the budget draft (including the General Account and the Special Account for Allocation and Transfer Taxes) of the next fiscal year. Based on the final negotiation, the MOHA formulates the Local Public Finance Program and the Local Bond Program that sets the volume and lenders agreed above. Also the MOF formulates the Fiscal Investment and Loan Program (FILP) that sets the underwriting to national and local bonds. Thus the Local Bond Program is a close relation to the FILP.

The Local Bond Program sets not only the volume of issuance but also the lenders of the bonds. The lenders consisted of the TFB of the Ministry of Finance, the Postal Life Insurance, the JFM, and private financial institutions, until 2000. The TFB funds and the Postal Life Insurance funds are called the government funds. Also the government funds and the JFM are called the Fiscal Investment and Loan (FIL) funds. Local governments can issue private placement bonds and publicly-subscribed bonds to the private sector.

As shown in Figure 3, the government funds occupy about 50%, the JFM occupies about 10%, and the private funds occupy about 40% of the total funds in the recent Local Bond Program. That is, the FIL funds occupy about 60% of the total fund. The TFB funds of the MOF lend to local governments the approved borrowing from government funds. The Postal Life Insurance Funds of the (former) Ministry of Posts and Telecommunications (the present Ministry of Public Management, Home Affairs, Posts and Telecommunications) also lends to local governments.

As mentioned above, not only the MOHA but also the MOF affect the approval of local bonds. In particular, the borrowing from the FIL funds is an important component of the approval. What local governments are permitted more issuance of local bonds and more borrowings from the FIL funds by the Minister of Home Affairs? We propose hypotheses on this in the next section.

[6] Ishihara (1976) mentions that the government funds (i.e. the FIL funds) are the best and safest funds for local governments, and he (the past Vice-Minister of the Home Affairs) hopes that borrowing from the FIL funds increase more and more (p.264).

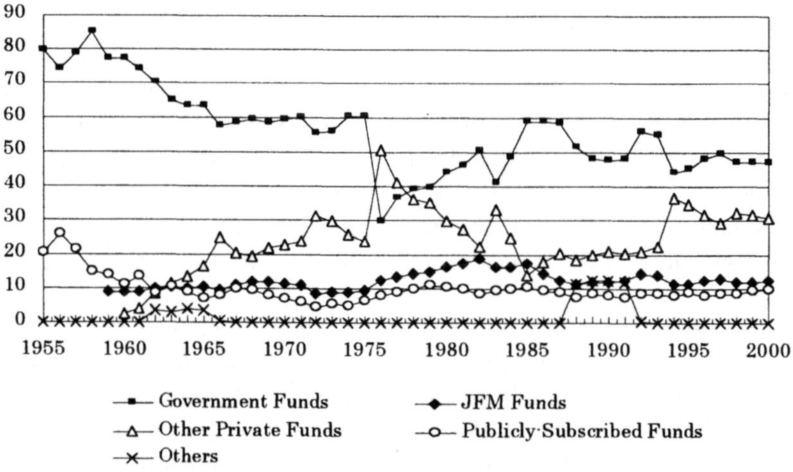

Figure 3. Composition of funds for the Local Bond Program

3. THE ROLE OF LOCAL BONDS PERMITS AND ITS HYPOTHESES

3.1 The role of Local Bonds Permits

How does the central government manage the System of Local Bonds Permits? Tanimoto and Ishii (1986) mention that the intents of the system of Local Bonds Permits are as follows: (1) maintenance of fiscal discipline of local finance, (2) adjustment of the difference between the local governments' demand for borrowing and funds available to them, and prevention of funds flowing only into larger or richer localities at the expense of smaller or poorer ones, (3) adjustment of revenues among the Local Taxes, the LAT, and the Local Bonds, (4) (implicit) guarantee on local bonds, and (5) unification of judgment in lending the FIL funds

These intents suggest that the central government distributes the FIL funds, which are at lower interest rates and longer maturity than private funds, to prefectures whose tax revenue is lower (Tanimoto and Ishii (1986) pp.60-61). They also suggest that permission for issuing local bonds has a close relation to allocation of the LAT, which promotes equality in local government revenue (Tanimoto and Ishii (1986) p.61). These affect the policy of Local Bonds Permits

All local governments borrow from the FIL funds and the private financial institutions by private placement loan. Some prefectures have issued publicly-subscribed bonds thorough security markets such as the Tokyo Stock Exchange. In prefectures, Tokyo, Osaka, and Hyogo have issued since FY 1952, Hokkaido, Kanagawa, Shizuoka, Aichi, Hiroshima, and Fukuoka have issued since FY 1973, Miyagi, Saitama, Chiba, and Kyoto have issued since FY 1975, Ibaraki, Niigata, and Nagano have issued since 1989. The others have never issued publicly-subscribed bonds in security markets.

In the above situation, we can guess that volume and lenders of local bonds are different among prefectures.[7] As a preparatory research, we view data on local bonds in each prefecture. First of all, we show the volume of prefectural bonds (in the ordinary account). The per cent distribution of prefectural bonds outstanding (= prefectural bonds outstanding in the prefecture / the total outstanding of all prefectural bonds) is shown in Table 1. We can confirm that Tokyo has the most, followed by Hokkaido, Osaka, and Hyogo. The above prefectures issue publicly-subscribed bonds. Similarly, the per cent distribution of borrowing outstanding from the FIL funds (= prefectural bonds outstanding in the prefecture / the total outstanding of all prefectural bonds) is shown in Table 2.[8] We can observe that Hokkaido has the most. Moreover, by the definition, a prefecture whose percentage in Table 1 is higher than that in Table 2, is one which has the ratio of borrowing outstanding from the FIL funds to the total funds is less than the average in each fiscal year. A bold figure in Table 2 denotes such a prefecture. Saitama, Chiba, Tokyo, Kanagawa, Shizuoka, Aichi, Shiga, Kyoto, Osaka, Hyogo, and Fukuoka, which are prefectures in urban area (and issuing their bonds at security markets), borrow less from the FIL funds.[9] In Figure 4, we show a time-series pass of the ratio of borrowing outstanding from the FIL funds to the total funds (= borrowing outstanding from the FIL funds / the total outstanding of prefectural bonds in each prefecture) in Hokkaido, Fukushima, Tokyo, Ishikawa, Osaka, and Okinawa, for example. The highest ratio of all prefectures is Okinawa, and the lowest ratio of all prefectures is Tokyo through 1975-1997. Black dots denote the

[7] As we will mention below, we use prefectural data. The reason is that we obtain prefectural data on finance and economy, especially lenders and maturity of prefectural bonds, but do not obtain municipal data.

[8] We would like to obtain data on this percentage in issuing. Unfortunately we cannot obtain it. Therefore we use the percentage of outstanding as a proxy.

[9] In Japan, prefectures in urban areas are Saitama, Chiba, Tokyo, Kanagawa, Aichi, Kyoto, Osaka, and Hyogo, and in addition, Shizuoka, Hiroshima, and Fukuokaif more broadly defined.

prefectures that cannot issue publicly-subscribed bonds, and white dots denote those prefectures that can issue publicly-subscribed bonds. As shown in Figure 4, a prefecture whose ratio of borrowing outstanding from the FIL funds to the total funds was high in previous years tends to face a higher ratio in later years.

Table 1. Per cent distribution of prefectural bonds outstanding

		1965	1970	1975	1980	1985	1990	1995	1998
1	Hokkaido	4.2%	3.8%	2.8%	4.5%	6.1%	7.5%	6.0%	6.1%
2	Aomori	1.4%	1.6%	1.4%	1.9%	1.9%	1.8%	1.5%	1.5%
3	Iwate	1.3%	1.1%	1.3%	1.7%	1.7%	1.8%	1.6%	1.8%
4	Miyagi	1.8%	1.7%	1.5%	1.6%	1.8%	2.1%	1.9%	1.9%
5	Akita	1.4%	1.4%	1.2%	1.7%	1.7%	1.8%	1.6%	1.6%
6	Yamagata	1.3%	1.1%	1.0%	1.5%	1.5%	1.6%	1.4%	1.4%
7	Fukushima	1.7%	1.5%	1.4%	1.8%	1.9%	1.9%	1.5%	1.6%
8	Ibaraki	2.1%	2.0%	1.4%	1.5%	1.5%	1.7%	1.7%	1.9%
9	Tochigi	1.3%	1.0%	0.9%	1.1%	1.2%	1.3%	1.3%	1.3%
10	Gumma	1.2%	1.0%	0.9%	1.3%	1.4%	1.4%	1.2%	1.2%
11	Saitama	1.6%	1.9%	1.8%	1.9%	2.5%	3.0%	3.3%	3.5%
12	Chiba	1.9%	2.1%	2.6%	2.5%	2.5%	2.7%	2.7%	2.8%
13	Tokyo	13.4%	17.8%	21.8%	17.5%	13.2%	9.6%	12.5%	11.3%
14	Kanagawa	1.4%	2.0%	3.6%	3.4%	3.7%	3.0%	3.6%	3.5%
15	Niigata	3.7%	4.1%	2.3%	2.6%	2.7%	2.7%	2.4%	2.5%
16	Toyama	2.1%	1.7%	1.2%	1.4%	1.5%	1.6%	1.4%	1.3%
17	Ishikawa	1.6%	1.6%	1.2%	1.2%	1.4%	1.4%	1.2%	1.2%
18	Fukui	1.5%	1.4%	1.0%	1.0%	0.9%	0.9%	1.0%	1.0%
19	Yamanashi	0.7%	0.7%	0.7%	0.9%	1.0%	1.1%	1.0%	1.0%
20	Nagano	2.7%	2.3%	1.7%	1.6%	2.1%	2.5%	2.6%	2.5%
21	Gifu	2.3%	1.7%	1.4%	1.4%	1.2%	1.3%	1.3%	1.5%
22	Shizuoka	3.7%	3.9%	3.0%	2.2%	2.2%	2.3%	2.6%	2.8%
23	Aichi	2.8%	2.3%	3.9%	3.8%	4.4%	4.6%	4.6%	4.5%
24	Mie	2.6%	1.6%	1.5%	1.2%	1.1%	1.1%	1.3%	1.3%
25	Shiga	1.1%	1.0%	1.1%	1.0%	1.0%	1.0%	1.1%	1.1%
26	Kyoto	1.5%	1.2%	1.5%	1.2%	1.4%	1.4%	1.6%	1.6%
27	Osaka	5.7%	7.8%	8.7%	7.0%	6.2%	5.1%	5.8%	5.7%
28	Hyogo	3.7%	4.5%	5.3%	4.6%	4.1%	3.9%	4.8%	5.0%
29	Nara	1.2%	1.0%	0.8%	0.7%	1.1%	1.3%	1.2%	1.2%
30	Wakayama	2.2%	1.4%	0.7%	0.9%	0.9%	1.0%	1.0%	1.0%
31	Tottori	0.9%	0.7%	0.6%	0.9%	0.9%	0.8%	0.7%	0.7%
32	Shimane	1.2%	0.9%	0.8%	1.2%	1.3%	1.4%	1.1%	1.2%

Table 1. (continued)

		1965	1970	1975	1980	1985	1990	1995	1998
33	Okayama	1.9%	1.8%	1.7%	1.4%	1.5%	1.8%	1.8%	1.6%
34	Hiroshima	2.4%	2.3%	2.0%	2.2%	2.0%	2.0%	1.9%	2.0%
35	Yamaguchi	2.0%	1.6%	1.4%	1.5%	1.5%	1.4%	1.3%	1.3%
36	Tokushima	1.1%	1.1%	0.9%	0.9%	0.9%	1.1%	1.1%	1.1%
37	Kagawa	0.9%	0.7%	0.5%	0.7%	0.8%	0.8%	0.9%	0.9%
38	Ehime	1.4%	1.1%	1.1%	1.2%	0.9%	0.8%	1.0%	1.1%
39	Kochi	1.5%	1.1%	1.0%	1.3%	1.4%	1.4%	1.2%	1.1%
40	Fukuoka	3.5%	3.9%	3.3%	3.3%	3.6%	3.5%	2.9%	2.8%
41	Saga	1.2%	0.9%	0.8%	1.0%	0.8%	0.9%	0.8%	0.8%
42	Nagasaki	1.2%	1.1%	1.2%	1.4%	1.5%	1.6%	1.5%	1.5%
43	Kumamoto	1.5%	1.1%	1.1%	1.6%	1.9%	2.2%	1.9%	1.8%
44	Oita	1.4%	1.1%	1.2%	1.3%	1.2%	1.3%	1.3%	1.3%
45	Miyazaki	1.5%	1.2%	1.0%	1.3%	1.4%	1.3%	1.1%	1.1%
46	Kagoshima	1.3%	1.4%	1.1%	1.7%	1.8%	2.1%	1.9%	1.9%
47	Okinawa	--	--	0.5%	0.6%	0.9%	1.2%	1.0%	0.9%

As of end of FY

Table 2. Per cent distribution of borrowing outstanding from the FIL funds (share of outstanding of the all prefecture)

		1965	1970	1975	1980	1985	1990	1995	1998
1	Hokkaido	5.3%	4.9%	4.6%	5.0%	6.2%	8.5%	7.9%	8.2%
2	Aomori	1.6%	2.0%	2.3%	2.5%	2.3%	2.4%	2.1%	2.0%
3	Iwate	1.4%	1.5%	1.6%	2.3%	2.4%	2.4%	2.4%	2.4%
4	Miyagi	**1.5%**	1.8%	1.7%	2.0%	2.0%	2.1%	2.1%	2.0%
5	Akita	1.8%	1.7%	1.9%	2.2%	2.2%	2.2%	1.9%	1.8%
6	Yamagata	1.7%	1.5%	1.7%	2.0%	2.1%	2.3%	2.1%	2.1%
7	Fukushima	2.0%	2.3%	2.4%	2.7%	2.7%	2.8%	2.4%	2.4%
8	Ibaraki	2.1%	2.5%	2.1%	2.3%	2.1%	2.4%	2.3%	2.4%
9	Tochigi	1.7%	1.3%	1.2%	1.5%	1.7%	1.7%	1.6%	1.6%
10	Gumma	1.6%	1.2%	1.1%	1.5%	1.8%	1.7%	1.5%	1.5%
11	Saitama	**1.6%**	1.9%	1.9%	2.0%	**2.3%**	**2.4%**	**2.7%**	**2.6%**
12	Chiba	2.0%	2.4%	2.7%	**2.3%**	**2.0%**	**1.9%**	**2.0%**	**1.9%**
13	Tokyo	**5.1%**	**5.4%**	**4.6%**	**2.4%**	**1.9%**	**1.2%**	**2.9%**	**3.0%**
14	Kanagawa	**1.0%**	**1.3%**	**1.7%**	**1.7%**	**2.1%**	**1.6%**	**1.9%**	**1.8%**
15	Niigata	4.3%	5.7%	4.2%	3.8%	3.6%	3.7%	3.4%	3.7%

Table 2. (continued)

		1965	1970	1975	1980	1985	1990	1995	1998
16	Toyama	2.6%	2.2%	1.8%	1.7%	1.6%	1.7%	1.6%	1.7%
17	Ishikawa	1.8%	1.9%	1.8%	1.8%	1.7%	1.5%	1.3%	1.4%
18	Fukui	2.0%	1.7%	1.4%	1.5%	1.3%	1.2%	1.2%	1.3%
19	Yamanashi	0.9%	1.0%	1.0%	1.4%	1.6%	1.5%	1.5%	1.5%
20	Nagano	3.0%	3.1%	2.6%	2.2%	3.2%	3.1%	3.1%	3.0%
21	Gifu	2.7%	2.3%	2.1%	2.0%	1.7%	1.8%	1.7%	1.8%
22	Shizuoka	**3.7%**	**3.8%**	3.6%	2.9%	2.4%	**2.1%**	**2.2%**	**2.2%**
23	Aichi	3.2%	2.5%	**3.0%**	**3.3%**	**4.0%**	**3.8%**	**3.7%**	**3.4%**
24	Mie	3.3%	2.3%	2.5%	2.1%	1.8%	1.7%	1.6%	1.7%
25	Shiga	1.4%	1.1%	1.3%	1.2%	1.2%	1.0%	**1.0%**	**1.1%**
26	Kyoto	1.8%	1.6%	1.7%	1.4%	**1.2%**	**1.2%**	**1.3%**	**1.4%**
27	Osaka	**2.4%**	**3.3%**	**3.8%**	**2.5%**	**2.7%**	**2.4%**	**3.2%**	**3.3%**
28	Hyogo	**3.5%**	4.8%	5.6%	**4.6%**	**3.2%**	**2.5%**	**3.5%**	**3.7%**
29	Nara	1.4%	1.1%	1.0%	1.0%	1.4%	1.6%	1.5%	1.4%
30	Wakayama	2.6%	1.7%	1.2%	1.1%	1.1%	1.2%	1.2%	1.2%
31	Tottori	0.9%	0.7%	0.8%	1.2%	1.2%	1.2%	1.0%	1.0%
32	Shimane	1.5%	1.3%	1.3%	1.6%	1.8%	1.9%	1.7%	1.6%
33	Okayama	2.2%	2.3%	2.1%	1.9%	1.7%	1.9%	2.1%	2.0%
34	Hiroshima	3.1%	3.0%	3.0%	2.8%	2.2%	2.1%	2.1%	2.2%
35	Yamaguchi	2.3%	2.3%	2.2%	2.0%	1.9%	1.8%	1.8%	1.9%
36	Tokushima	1.4%	1.2%	1.3%	1.4%	1.3%	1.4%	1.3%	1.4%
37	Kagawa	1.1%	1.0%	0.9%	1.1%	1.2%	1.1%	1.0%	1.0%
38	Ehime	1.6%	1.6%	1.5%	1.8%	1.2%	1.1%	1.2%	1.3%
39	Kochi	1.7%	1.4%	1.7%	2.0%	2.0%	1.9%	1.8%	1.7%
40	Fukuoka	3.6%	4.6%	4.1%	4.1%	4.0%	**3.4%**	**2.9%**	**2.8%**
41	Saga	1.3%	1.2%	1.3%	1.4%	1.2%	1.2%	1.2%	1.2%
42	Nagasaki	1.6%	1.4%	1.3%	1.5%	1.9%	1.9%	1.9%	1.6%
43	Kumamoto	1.7%	1.3%	1.7%	2.5%	2.8%	2.9%	3.1%	3.0%
44	Oita	1.5%	1.6%	1.6%	1.8%	1.8%	1.8%	1.7%	1.6%
45	Miyazaki	1.9%	1.7%	1.6%	1.9%	1.9%	1.9%	1.8%	1.7%
46	Kagoshima	1.5%	1.7%	2.0%	2.6%	2.6%	2.9%	2.7%	2.8%
47	Okinawa	--	--	1.2%	1.4%	1.8%	1.9%	1.8%	1.6%

As of end of FY

Bold: Prefectures which have the ratio of borrowing outstanding from the FIL funds to the total funds less than the average in each fiscal year.

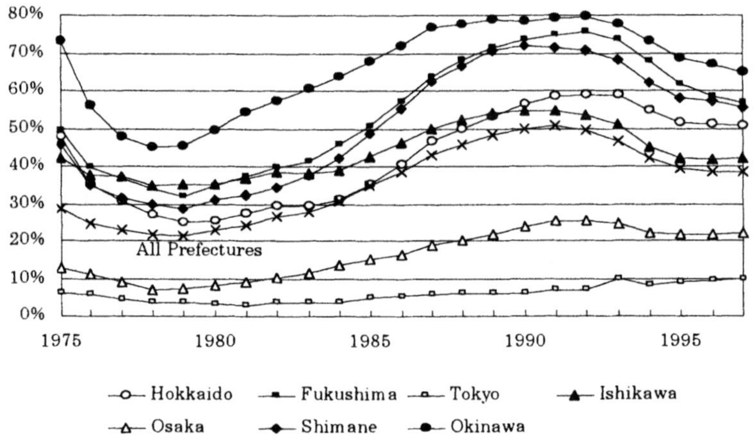

Figure 4. Ratio of borrowing from the FIL funds to the total funds

From this and the fact that the FIL funds are the funds with a lower interest rate and longer maturity, we can surmise that a prefecture, which cannot issue publicly-subscribed bonds, tends to borrow more from the FIL bonds. If this tendency dominates, the central government intentionally gives an implicit subsidy for interest payment to the prefecture (that is a rural area). These rural prefectures cannot issue publicly-subscribed bonds and do not face a financial discipline in the security markets. Because of this, the prefecture may lose an incentive to improve their fiscal situation, as the prefectures can borrow with a low interest rate and long maturity without striving to search for lenders. Whether this is actually the case requires further investigations.

Now, we discuss the fiscal situation faced by each prefecture. We compare indicators on the interest rate and outstanding amount of local bonds to investigate whether a fiscal and financial discipline exists. On the interest rate, the terms for borrowing from the FIL funds are the same for all prefectures. However if the volume and timing of borrowing from the FIL fund, and the terms for borrowing from private funds, is different among prefectures, then the effective interest rate is different. We show the (nominal) effective interest rate (= interest payment / the total outstanding of prefectural bonds as of end of the previous year) in Figure 5. The rate in some prefectures is shown in Figure 5. In Figure 5, wedraw its time-series pass in the same prefectures in Figure 4. The point on the upper line denotes the rate that is the highest effective interest rate in the year. And the point on the lower line denotes the rate that is the lowest effective interest rate in the year.

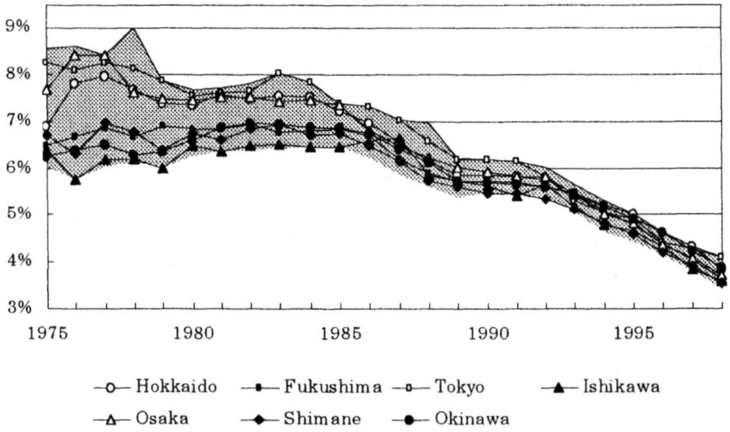

Figure 5. Effective interest rates

The correlation of the (nominal) effective interest rate with the ratio of prefectural bonds outstanding to Gross Prefectural Domestic Product (GPDP) is shown in Figure 6. The values in Figure 6 are the annual average in the sample period (FY 1975-1997 in Figure 6-1, and FY 1990-1997 in Figure 6-2). A number in the figures, hereafter, is one of each prefecture in Table 1. We observe a negative correlation of the effective interest rate with the ratio of prefectural bonds outstanding to GPDP in Figure 6.

We also show the correlation of the (nominal) effective interest rate with the ratio of borrowing outstanding from the FIL funds to the total funds in Figure 7. We observe a negative correlation of the effective interest rate with the ratio of borrowing outstanding from the FIL funds to total funds. The correlation of the effective interest rate with maturity structure of local bonds is shown in Figure 8. As mentioned above, maturity of the FIL funds is relatively long (the longest is 30 years), but for private funds is almost 7-10 years. We obtain data on maturity of local bonds outstanding, especially volume of bonds that will be redeemed within 5 years from 1975 (within 6 years from 1977) in official statistics (The Ministry of Home Affairs, "Financial Index Table by Prefecture").[10] We can regard the ratio of bonds redeemed within 5 years to the total bonds (= bonds that will be redeemed within 5 years / the total outstanding of prefectural bonds in each prefecture) as an indicator of maturity. An increase in the ratio means that the maturity of the prefecture shortens. As shown in Figure 8, the effective interest rate

[10] We cannot obtain data volume of bonds that will be redeemed after over 6 years from 1975 (over 7 years from 1977) in official statistics.

has a negative correlation with the ratio of bonds redeemed within 5 years to the total bonds. The ratio of bonds redeemed within 5 years to the total bonds is lower and the effective interest rate is higher in urban areas. A prefecture whose ratio of borrowing outstanding from the FIL funds to the total funds is lower doesn't face a higher ratio of bonds redeemed within 5 years to the total bonds, as shown in Figure 7 and 8.

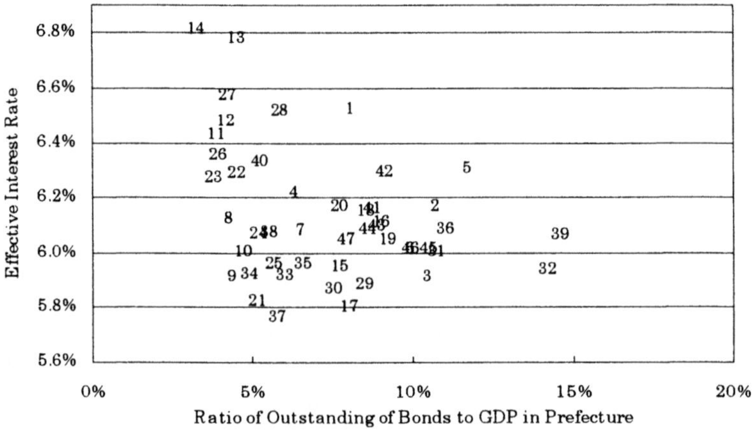

Figure 6.1. Effective interest rate and local bonds outstanding: FY1975-1997 (average)

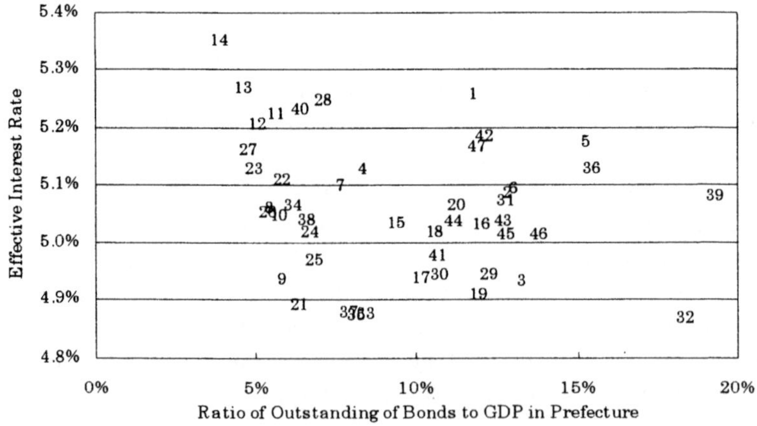

Figure 6.2. Effective interest rate and local bonds outstanding: FY1990-1997 (average)

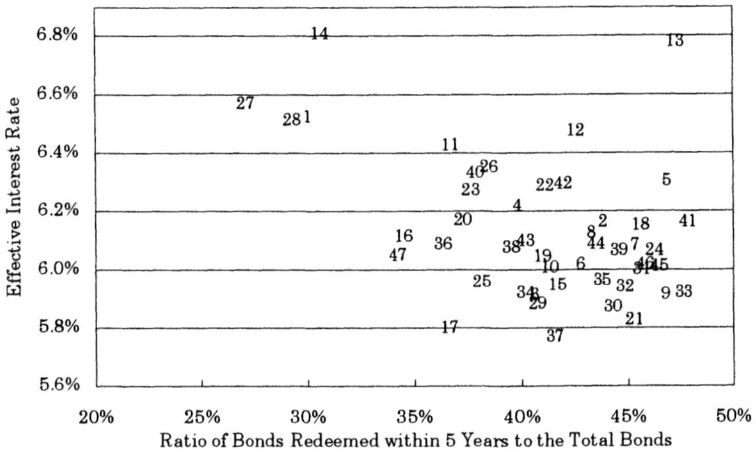

Figure 7.1. Effective interest rate and maturity structure: FY1975-1997 (average)

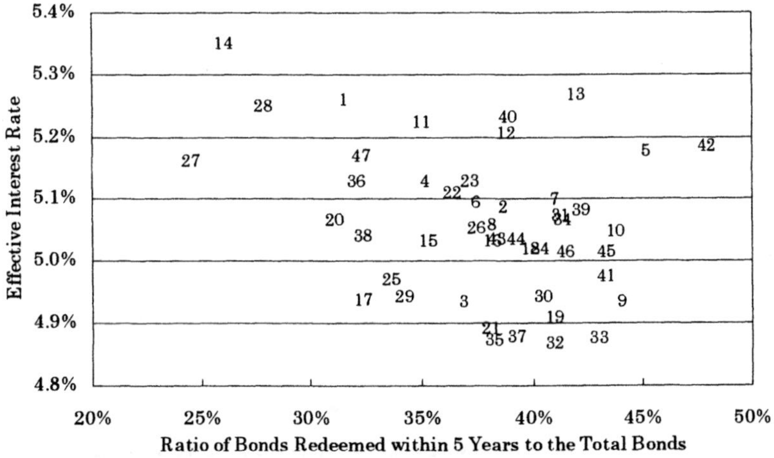

Figure 7.2. Effective interest rate and maturity structure: FY1990-1997 (average)

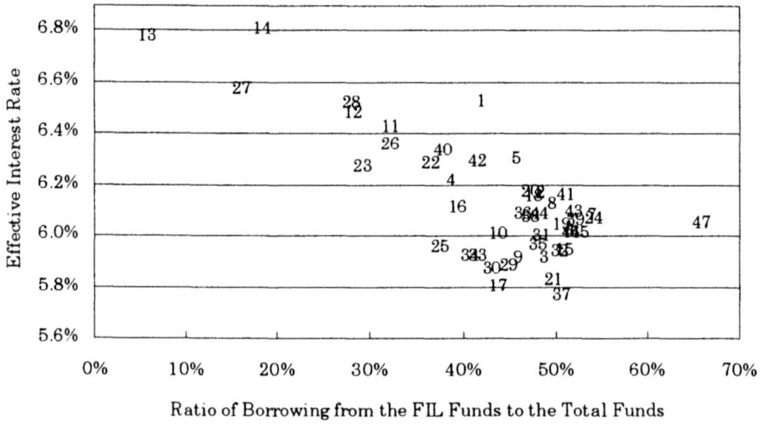

Figure 8.1. Effective interest rate and borrowing from the FIL funds: FY1975-1997 (average)

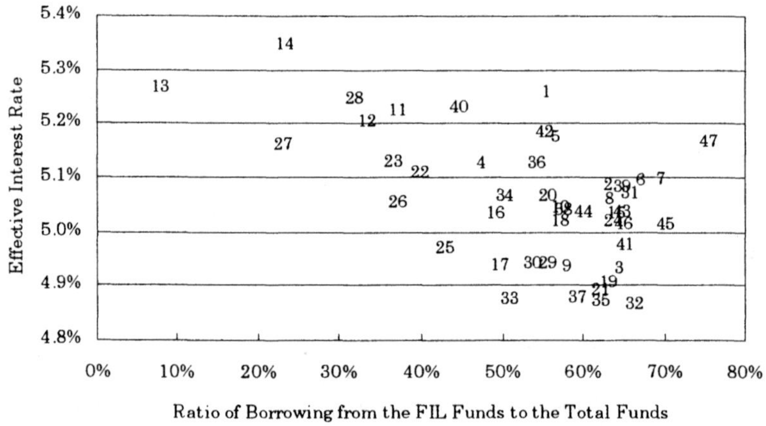

Figure 8.2. Effective interest rate and borrowing from the FIL funds: FY1990-1997 (average)

3.2 Hypotheses to assess the system

We consider hypotheses in econometric tests from the facts mentioned in Section 3.1. We also discuss hypotheses from economic theories.

First of all, we set a hypothesis that a prefecture whose financial capability index is lower, that is, tax revenue is lower, has a higher ratio of borrowing outstanding from the FIL funds to total funds. A prefecture whose financial capability index is lower collects so few tax revenue that it needs to issue more local bonds even if it obtains revenue from the LAT and the National Government Disbursement. If the central government permits more issue of local borrowing from the FIL funds to such a prefecture, then its borrowing outstanding from the FIL fundsincreases.

Secondly, we set a hypothesis that a prefecture whose ratio of borrowing outstanding from the FIL funds to the total funds is higher faces a lower effective interest rate. The reason is that lending rates for the FIL funds are intentionally keptlower than for private funds.

Thirdly, we set a hypothesis that a prefecture whose ratio of borrowing outstanding from the FIL funds to the total funds is higher in previous years still has the higher ratio in later years. This hypothesis is deduced from intents of the System of Local Bonds Permits mentioned above and an intuitive observation in Figure 4.

We infer these three hypotheses from properties including the System of Local Bonds Permits. On the other hand, we consider hypotheses that are deduced from the motivation that private financial institutions turn a profit on the lending to prefectures. We propose hypotheses as follows.

Fourthly, we set a hypothesis that a prefecture, whose ratio of prefectural bonds outstanding to GPDP is higher, faces a higher effective interest rate. As suggested by Alesina, De Broeck, Prati, and Tabellini (1992), which analyze the relationship among interest rates of national bonds, and economic and fiscal situation among OECD countries. A government that increases outstanding bonds to economic scale may face a higher interest rate, because the possibility of default in such a government becomes higher and lenders require a risk premium.

Fifthly, we set a hypothesis that a prefecture whose maturity of prefectural bonds shortens faces a higher effective interest rate. As Missale and Blanchard (1994) have mentioned, if government bonds are increasing, a shortening maturity means that there is a perception that lenders (especially private financial institutions) will not lend with longer maturity to a government that may default on its borrowings in the near future. Such a government may borrow with only high interest rate, because lenders require a risk premium.

Finally, we set a hypothesis that a prefecture that borrows more from private funds faces a lower effective interest rate. Bonds of such a prefecture circulate more among private financial institutions. These lenders require a lower liquidity premium to lend to such a prefecture, and its effective interest rate is lower. We use an indicator of volume of circulation as the per cent distribution of borrowing outstanding from private funds (= (the total outstanding of prefectural bonds – borrowing outstanding from the FIL funds in each prefecture) / the sum of borrowing outstanding from private funds in all prefectures) we examine whether the effective interest rate is lower as the percentage increases.

We analyze the above six hypotheses in the next section.

4. EMPIRICAL RESULTS

4.1 Unit root tests in panel data

We try an econometric analysis of the System of Local Bond Permits using data on prefectural finance. We can obtain these data, especially maturity of prefectural bonds, from FY 1975. We analyze panel data on prefectural finance and economy from 1975 because these time-series data are too small to analyze each prefecture. Also we cannot get data on municipal finance and economy, especially lenders and maturity of municipal bonds.

Before the panel analysis, we examine unit root tests in this panel data (47 prefecture, FY 1976-1997). A unit root test in panel data is developed by Levin and Lin (1992, 1993). Levin and Lin (1992) show Monte Carlo results on the finite-sample properties of the unit roott-statistics.

If we set the following (standard) dynamic model of a series x_{it} (individual $i = 1, 2, \ldots, N$, and time period $t = 1, 2, \ldots, T$) for panel data

$$x_{it} = \rho x_{it-1} + \lambda_0 + \lambda_1 t + a_{0i} + a_{1t} + \omega_{it}$$

where λ_0: the intercept, a_{0i}: the individual-specific effect, a_{1t}: the time-specific effect, and ω_{it}: the error term (i.i.d.), then, as Nickell (1981) has shown, the least square estimator of ρ is underestimated when this time-series periods are small in number. Therefore a unit root test (null hypothesis: $\rho = 1$) in this model using (standard) t-distribution gives a wrong result.

Levin and Lin (1992) obtain statistics of unit root tests (null hypothesis: $\rho = 1$) of various models. We use the following model to test

$$x_{it} = \rho x_{it-1} + a_{0i} + \omega_{it} \qquad \omega_{it} \sim \mathrm{N}(0,1), \text{ i.i.d..}$$

We eliminate the time trend in the above model because the estimator of time trend is not significant in the dynamic model of almost all the series used in this paper. Levin and Lin (1992) present the unit root t-statistic of the above model in panel data as follows. When N =50 and T =25, 1 percent critical value is -10.89, 5 percent critical value is -10.35, and 10 percent critical value is -10.06. In our data, N =47 and T =22 (FY 1976-1997).

We use the following data: The real effective interest rate (= nominal effective interest rate – deflator of Gross Prefectural Domestic Product at constant 1990 prices: ri), the ratio of prefectural bonds outstanding to GPDP (by), the percentage changes in ratio of prefectural bonds outstanding to GPDP (dby), the ratio of borrowing outstanding from the FIL funds to the total funds (sgpb), the ratio of primary balance in prefectural finance to GPDP (pby), the financial capability index (index), the ratio of bonds redeemed within 5 years to the total bonds(short), the per cent distribution of borrowing outstanding from private funds (shmb), the real growth rate of prefectural bonds outstanding (grrb), the real GPDP growth rate (gry), the rate of population increase (grpop), the real growth rate of tax revenue (grtax), the active job openings ratio (e), the proportion of the population aged under 14 (p14), the proportion of the population aged over 65 (p65), the real GPDP per capita (ryp), and the real tax revenue per capita (rtp) . We test unit roots of the above series, and obtain these unit root t-values are shown in Table 3. ** in Table 3 indicates the rejection of null hypothesis, that is, the series has a unit root.

4.2 Estimation of simultaneous equations

In this section, we build a model to investigate the system and role of Local Bonds Permits in Japan. We set the following simultaneous equations to examine hypothesesmentionedin Section 3.

$$\mathrm{sgpb}_{it} = \alpha_i + \beta_0 \mathrm{t} + \beta_1 \mathrm{sgpb}_{it-1} + \beta_2 \mathrm{index}_{it} + \beta_3 \mathrm{pby}_{it} + \beta_4 \mathrm{gry}_{it} + \beta_5 \mathrm{e}_{it} + u_{it}$$
$$\mathrm{ri}_{it} = \gamma_i + \delta_0 \mathrm{t} + \delta_1 \mathrm{dby}_{it} + \delta_2 \mathrm{sgpb}_{it} + \delta_3 \mathrm{short}_{it} + \delta_4 \mathrm{pby}_{it} + \delta_5 \mathrm{gry}_{it} + \delta_6 \mathrm{e}_{it} + v_{it}$$
$$\mathrm{pby}_{it} = \zeta_i + \eta_0 \mathrm{t} + \eta_1 \mathrm{ri}_{it} + \eta_2 \mathrm{sgpb}_{it} + \eta_3 \mathrm{gry}_{it} + \eta_4 \mathrm{e}_{it} + \varepsilon_{it}$$

where u_{it}, v_{it}, and ε_{it} denote error terms in each equation, respectively. We call the set of these three equations simultaneous equations (I). The first equation of (I) expresses what prefectures are permitted to borrow from the FIL funds by the MOHA. It includes the first hypothesis (index), the third hypothesis (sgpb in previous fiscal year) in Section 3. In addition, it also includes the ratio of primary balance in prefectural finance to GPDP (pby), which means how closely the permission of the Minister of Home Affairs responds to the situation of prefectural finance.

Table 3. Unit root tests

		Test statistic	
Real effective interest rate	ri	-61.423	**
Ratio of prefectural bonds outstanding to GPDP	by	24.889	
Percentage changes in ratio of prefectural bonds outstanding to GPDP	dby	-17.563	**
Ratio of borrowing outstanding from the FIL funds to the total funds	sgpb	-50.281	**
Ratio of primary balance in prefectural finance to GPDP	pby	-12.638	**
Financial capability index	index	-83.853	**
Ratio of bonds redeemed within 5 years to the total bonds	short	-59.789	**
Per cent distribution of borrowing outstanding from private funds	shmb	-149.012	**
Real growth rate of prefectural bonds outstanding	grrb	-31.851	**
Real GPDP growth rate	gry	-43.671	**
Rate of population increase	grpop	-25.919	**
Real growth rate of tax revenue	grtax	-38.417	**
Active job openings ratio	e	-35.132	**
Proportion of the population aged under 14	p14	-7.480	
Proportion of the population aged over 65	p65	25.712	
Real GPDP per capita	ryp	-4.133	
Real tax revenue per capita	rtp	-17.391	**

** and * denote significance at 1% and 5% level, respectively.

The second equation expresses factors to determine the effective interest rate faced by each prefecture in each period. It includes the second hypothesis (sgpb), the fourth hypothesis (by), and the fifth hypothesis (short) in Section 3.2. Moreover we add the ratio of primary balance in prefectural finance to GPDP (pby) as an independent variable in this equation. The reason for this addition is that we accept the fact deduced by Caselli, Giovannini, and Lane (1998), that the effective interest rate correlates with primary balance in the government budget constraint. We use dby, which is the first difference of by, in this equation. The reason why we use not by_{it} but dby_{it} is that the hypothesis that by_{it} has a unit root in panel data is not rejected as shown in Table 3.

Finally, the third equation implies the management of prefectural finance, especially primary balance. We use the effective interest rate (ri), the ratio of borrowing outstanding from the FIL funds to the total funds (sgpb), and the real GPDP growth rate (gry) as independent variables.[11] The effective interest rate affects debt expenditure (interest payment), and affects primary balance. As the effective interest rate is higher, debt expenditure increases. Then expenditures excluding debt expenditure decrease and the primary balance is improved when the tax revenue and bond issues cannot substantially increase further.

We add the real GPDP growth rate (gry) and the active job openings ratio (e) as independent variables to eliminate heterogeneity of prefectures. $sgpb_{it}$, ri_{it}, and pby_{it} are endogenous variables in the simultaneous equations (I). We use Baltagi (1981)'s (one-way) error components three-stage least squares (EC3SLS) to estimate the simultaneous equations in panel data.[12] Instrumental variables in the estimation are, as Baltagi (1995) has shown, all exogenous variables in the simultaneous equations. We present the results of estimation of the simultaneous equations (I) in Table 4. Incidentally, we also add the rate of population increase (grpop) as independent variables in each equation of the simultaneous equations (I) to eliminate heterogeneity of prefectures. We call these simultaneous equations simultaneous equations (II). We also estimate the simultaneous equations (II), and report the result in Table 4. As shown in Table 4, the estimators of coefficients of the rate of population increase (grpop) are not significant in the first and second equations. Therefore we explain an interpretation of the estimation using the result of the simultaneous equations(I).

As shown in Table 4, we obtain the result that the first and third hypotheses in Section 3.2 are supported in the first equation of the simultaneous equations (I). Moreover, we confirm that the ratio of primary

[11] Variables with respect to tax revenue are important to analyze the primary balance. We use the real growth rate of tax revenue (grtax) in our estimation, but the estimator of coefficient of grtax is not significant. Therefore we don't include grtax in our estimation.

[12] This 'one-way' implies individual effect.

balance in prefectural finance to GPDP has a positive correlation with the ratio of borrowing outstanding from the FIL funds to the total funds. This positive correlation means that the central government permits more borrowings from the FIL funds, when the ratio of primary balance in prefectural finance to GPDP becomes worse. The reason is that the prefectures with a worse financial situation issue more bonds in the fiscal year but the private financial institutions don't want to lend more to the prefectures. If the policy is continued, prefectures lose an incentive to improve their fiscal situation (ex. reducing issuance of local bonds), because the prefectures can borrow with a low interest rate and long maturity by the permission without having to search for lenders. It suggests that the permission of borrowings from the FIL funds doesn't work for maintenance of fiscal discipline of local finance.

Table 4. Estimations of simultaneous equations
Method: EC3SLS
Sample: FY1976-1997, 47 prefectures

Simultaneous equations	(I)	(II)	(III)
NOB	1034	1034	1034
	Dependent variable: sgpb		
Independent variables			
sgpb (previous year)	0.781	0.746	0.781
	(43.224)	(40.532)	(43.159)
index	-0.113	-0.020	-0.113
	(-8.141)	(-1.306)	(-8.123)
pby	7.044	6.857	7.057
	(13.399)	(12.106)	(13.391)
gry	0.124	0.121	0.124
	(3.290)	(3.261)	(3.286)
e	-0.019	-0.013	-0.019
	(-3.584)	(-2.377)	(-3.587)
grpop		-0.721	
		(-1.309)	
time trend	0.003	0.003	0.003
	(9.696)	(7.700)	(9.702)

Table 4. (continued)

Simultaneous equations	(I)	(II)	(III)
	Dependent variable: ri		
Independent variables			
dby	1.207	1.167	1.202
	(8.979)	(8.007)	(8.934)
sgpb	-0.073	-0.088	-0.074
	(-6.424)	(-7.272)	(-6.444)
short	0.016	0.019	0.016
	(3.005)	(3.250)	(2.988)
shmb			0.009
			(0.248)
pby	4.336	4.356	4.342
	(17.282)	(16.574)	(17.276)
gry	0.328	0.324	0.327
	(11.492)	(11.176)	(11.454)
e	-0.035	-0.033	-0.035
	(-14.157)	(-12.768)	(-14.133)
grpop		0.259	
		(0.845)	
time trend	0.003	0.003	0.003
	(17.889)	(17.208)	(17.940)
	Dependent variable: pby		
Independent variables			
ri	0.268	0.253	0.268
	(13.522)	(12.002)	(13.482)
sgpb	0.027	0.030	0.027
	(8.299)	(8.923)	(8.319)
gry	-0.070	-0.066	-0.070
	(-7.632)	(-7.202)	(-7.635)
e	0.009	0.009	0.009
	(13.613)	(12.207)	(13.632)
grpop		-0.178	
		(-2.034)	
time trend	-0.001	-0.001	-0.001
	(-14.746)	(-15.860)	(-14.721)

We get the result that the second, fourth, and fifth hypotheses in Section 3.2 are supported in the second equation of the simultaneous equations (I).

In the third equation of the simultaneous equations (I), we observe the ratio of primary balance in prefectural finance to GPDP has a significant positive correlation with the real (effective) interest rate. It implies that as the effective interest rate is higher, debt expenditure increases, then expenditures excluding debt expenditure decrease and primary balance is improved when the tax revenue and bond issue cannot increase. We also obtain a significantly positive correlation of the ratio of primary balance in prefectural finance to GPDP with the ratio of borrowing outstanding from the FIL funds to the total funds. It means the following situation. The terms for borrowing from the FIL funds are better for prefectures because the borrowings from FIL funds are lower interest rates than private funds. Then the prefectures tend to follow the guidance of the MOHA in order to be permitted more borrowings from the FIL funds by the MOHA. As mentioned above, the MOHA doesn't permit prefectures with higher debt expenditure ratios to issue local bonds.. Thus the prefecture tries to reduce the debt expenditure ratio (used as permission to issue local bonds), and improve their primary balance.

Moreover, we observe that the real GPDP growth rate has a significant positive correlation with the ratio of primary balance in prefectural finance to GPDP. We discuss the interpretation of this correlation. As the real GPDP growth rate rises, prefectural tax revenue increases. On the other hand, the real GPDP growth rate rises, as the prefecture increases expenditures for public investments. If the former dominates the latter, primary balance in prefectural finance is improved. If the latter dominates the former, primary balance in prefectural finance becomes worse. Therefore, the positive correlation of the real GPDP growth rate with the ratio of primary balance in prefectural finance to GPDP means that prefectural tax revenue increases and primary balance is improved when the real GPDP growth rate rises for some reasons.[13]

Lastly, we add only the per cent distribution of borrowing outstanding from private funds (shmb) in the second equation of simultaneous equations (I) to investigate the sixth hypothesis in Section 3.2. We call the equations simultaneous equations (III). The result of estimation is shown in Table 4. As shown in Table 4, the estimator of the coefficient of shmb is not significant. It means that the sixth hypothesis is not supported. The other estimators in the simultaneous equations (III) are the same as those in the

[13] This positive correlation means that the ratio of primary balance in prefectural finance to GPDP is improved when GPDP increases more than the primary deficits in prefectural finance as well as the primary balance are improved. We obtain the same result, however, when we use primary balance to total expenditure in prefectural finance for pbyit as the dependent variable. Thus we conclude that the interpretation is relevant.

simultaneous equations (I). In this sense, we see the result of the simultaneous equations (I) is robust.

5. CONCLUDING REMARKS

From the result in Section 4, we conclude that the System of Local Bonds Permits works as a policy tool of fiscal equalization, however, borrowing from private financial institutions works as financial discipline as it is harder for prefectures with worse financial situation to borrow with lower interest rates. The detailed conclusion is as follows.

First of all, a prefecture whose financial capability index is lower, that is, tax revenue is fewer, has a higher ratio of borrowing outstanding from the FIL funds to the total funds. Secondly, a prefecture whose ratio of borrowing outstanding from the FIL funds to the total funds is higher faces a lower effective interest rate. Thirdly, a prefecture whose ratio of borrowing outstanding from the FIL funds to the total funds is higher in previous year still has a higher ratio in later years. Fourthly, a prefecture whose ratio of prefectural bonds outstanding to GPDP is higher faces a higher effective interest rate. Fifthly, a prefecture whose maturity of prefectural bonds shortens faces a higher effective interest rate

These suggest that the permission of borrowings from the FIL funds doesn't work for maintenance of fiscal discipline of local finance. However, borrowing from private financial institutions works as a financial discipline as it is harder for prefectures with worse financial situation to borrow with lower interest rates. The reason is that private financial institutions cannot profitably lend with lower interest rates and longer maturity to the prefectures with worse financial situations. The FIL funds are managed by the central government, and are, by law, not required to operate at a profit. We also observe that prefectures whose ratio of primary balance in prefectural finance to GPDP become worse, issue more bonds but as they cannot fully obtain revenue by borrowings from only private funds, then they heavily depend on borrowing from the FIL funds

We assess the system from the above analysis as follows. Under the System of Local Bonds Permits, the central government, especially the HOMA, makes much of the intention to adjust the difference between the local governments' demand for borrowing and funds available for them, and to prevent funds flowing only into larger or richer localities at the expense of smaller or poorer ones These were among the intentions identified in Tanimoto and Ishii (1986). From the first and second hypotheses supported by our analysis, we conclude that the central government tends to distribute the FIL funds with lower interest rates to a prefecture whose financial capability index is lower, and intentionally gives an implicit subsidy for interest payment to rural prefectures, that is, an interregional transfer from a prefecture in an urban area, which pays higher interest rates, to the prefecture in a rural area. Moreover, the above prefecture in a rural area cannot issue publicly-subscribed bonds and doesn't face a financial discipline in security markets. The permission of borrowings from the FIL funds doesn't work for maintenance of fiscal discipline of local finance.

We also conclude that borrowing from private financial institutions works as a financial discipline as it is harder for prefectures with worse financial situation to borrow with lower interest rates. From the fourth and fifth hypotheses supported by the analysis in Section 4, a prefecture whose ratio of prefectural bonds outstanding to GPDP is higher than that in previous year or whose maturity of local bonds shortens faces a higher effective interest rate. It suggests the policy implication that the central government decreases and repeals direct borrowing from the FIL funds, and makes local governments borrow more from private funds, because an increase in borrowings from private financial institutions substituted for the FIL funds strengthens financial discipline.

We can consider the other factor that the effective interest rate of a prefecture is higher. For example, we can point out the timing of issuance: The effective interest rate of a prefecture which issue more in periods with tightening monetary policy (higher interest rates) is higher than that of a prefecture which issue less in the periods, if the other conditions are the same in both prefectures. Monetary policy affects an interest rate in issuing local bonds, that is, the interest rate of local bonds becomes higher when monetary policy tightens. For instance, Japanese monetary policy tightened in the middle of 1970s, the first half of the 1980s, and the early 1990s, as shown in Figure 9.

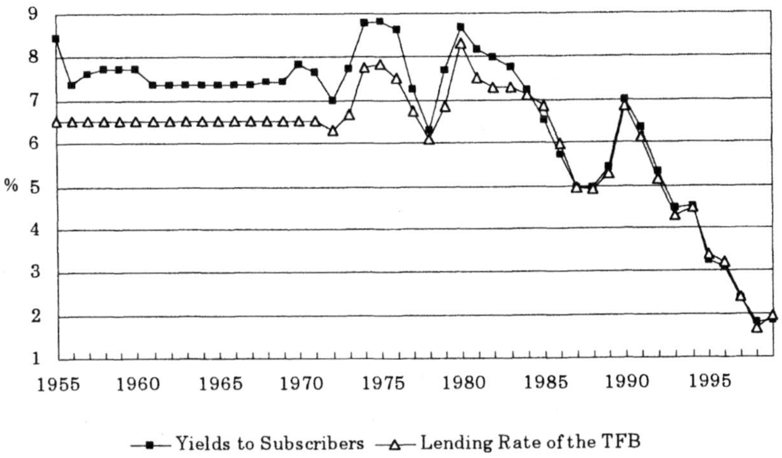

Figure 9. Interest rates of local bonds

On the other hand, we show (real) issuance of prefectural bonds in Figure 10. The figures in Figure 10 are the following values: Nominal issuance of prefectural bonds is deflated by the GPDP deflator, and normalized such that real issuance in 1975 is equal to unity in each prefecture shown in Figure 4 and 5. As shown in Figure 10, prefectures in rural areas issued more in the middle of the 1970s and the first half of the 1980s, but prefectures in urban area issued less than before the period. Prefectures that are not shown in Figure 10 are the same. It suggests that the effective interest rates of prefectures in rural areas tend to become higher than those of prefectures in urban areas.

As shown in Figure 6, 7, and 8, however, the effective interest rates of prefectures in rural areas are lower than those of prefectures in urban areas. It means that the effective interest rates are not directly affected by the timing of issuance, though this is intuitive. We don't include the timing of issuance in the analysis in Section 4. We needs more detailed estimation including this factor. This is a subject for further research.

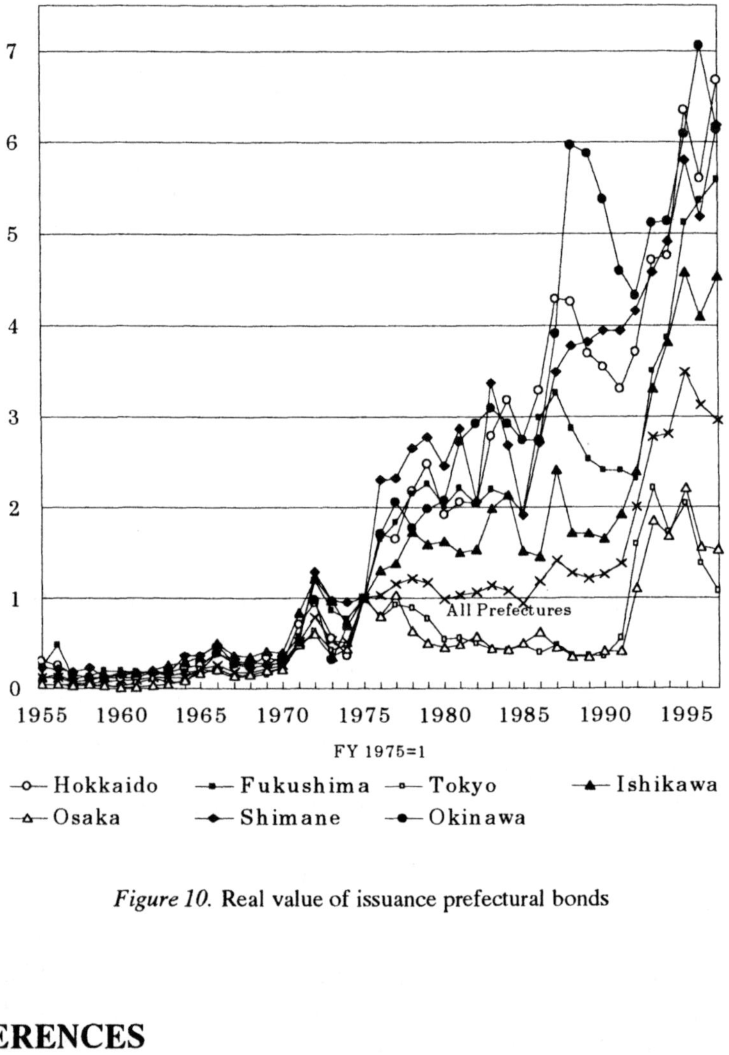

Figure 10. Real value of issuance prefectural bonds

REFERENCES

Alesina, A., M. De Broeck, A. Prati, and G. Tabellini, 1992, Default risk on government debt in OECD countries, *Economic Policy* 428-463.

Baltagi, B.H., 1981, Simultaneous equations with error components, *Journal of Econometrics* 17, 189-200.

Baltagi, B.H., 1995, *Econometrics Analysis of Panel Data*, John Wiley & Sons.

Caselli, F., A. Giovannini, and T. Lane, 1997, Fiscal discipline and the cost of public debt service: Some estimates for OECD countries, *mimeo*.

Doi, T., 2000, *Political Economy of Japanese Local Finance*, Toyo Keizai Inc (in Japanese).

Doi, T. and T. Nakazato, 1998, The sustainability of national and local government deficits in Japan, *Financial Review* 47, 76-105 (in Japanese).

Ishihara, N. ed., 1976, *Recent Theory of Management of Local Public Finance*, Gyosei (in Japanese).

Levin, A, and C.-F. Lin, 1992, Unit root tests in panel data: Asymptotic and finite-sample properties, *Discussion Paper* 92-23, University of California, San Diego.

Levin, A. and C.-F. Lin, 1993, Unit root tests in panel data: New result, *Discussion Paper* 93-56, University of California, San Diego.

Missale, A. and O.J. Blanchard, 1994, The debt burden and debt maturity, *American Economic Review* 84, 309-319.

Nakano, H., 2000, The system of Local Bonds Permits and local expenditures, in T. Ihori, R.R. Kato, H. Nakano, T. Nakazato, T. Doi, and S. Sato, *Economic Analysis of Budget Deficits*, *Economic Analysis, Shiten Series* 16, 139-168 (in Japanese).

Naruse, N. and Y. Isozaki, 1997, *The Local Administration in Japan*, Gyosei.

Nickell, 1981, Biases in dynamic models with fixed effects, *Econometrica* 49, 1417-1426.

Shibata, T. ed., 1993, *Japan's Public Sector: How the Government Is Financed*, University of Tokyo Press.

Takayori, S., 1988, *Recent Theory of Local Bonds*, Keiso Shobo (in Japanese).

Tanimoto, M. and R. Ishii, 1986, *Lectures on the Local Administration* 8, Dai-ichi Hoki (in Japanese).

Chapter 9

Local Governments

1. INTRODUCTION

Many local governments are in crisis. Their deficits are dramatically increasing. The outstanding amount of bonds, which was 52 trillion yen at the end of 1990 FY, is growing at an annual rate of almost 13% on average, and reached 100 trillion yen in 1996 FY.

Why is the amount of local government's bonds exploding? There are several restrictions placed upon the issuance of bonds by rule or codes, so their deficits or bond-issue should be under control.

One of the most important rules is that local governments are allowed to issue bonds only for financing capital expenditure, not for ordinary operations and they have to obtain prior permission from the central government.

In addition to these requirements, there is a ceiling for bond-debt outstanding, which is expected to suppress excess deficits. Local government must control the outstanding amount of bonds appropriately under its ceiling. If they don't, they cannot issue bonds and are put under central government control

This chapter shows that despite of various political rules and current codes to protect a healthy budget, they have still too much incentive to issue bonds.

The most important factor is the existence of grants that promote bond issues. For the last decade, the Japanese economy has been in a long recession and the central government has provided measures to promote the capital expenditures of local governments. In particular, the public investment program known as "the independent local public investment project" is one of the major policies in economic development programs. When conducting this project, local governments issue bonds and obtain grants for financing construction costs and interest payments. In Japan there are many local governments with little tax revenue, and they have heavily relied on central government for funds. Under these circumstances, executing a public investment project is preferable to ordinary operations for local governments with low revenues. They may be inclined to get revenues by conducting capital expenditure, even if there is no need for capital. It implies that the allocation of resources in local public finance is distorted.

The results presented here provide considerable evidence of the relation between the subsidies and capital expenditures by local governments. In section 2, we present the model of local government behavior, and in section 3, confirm the predictions of the model. Section 4 concludes this chapter.

2. CAPITAL EXPENDITURE AND BOND-DEBT CEILING IN JAPAN

The structure of financing capital expenditures has dramatically changed in local governments. There are two kinds of local public investment project, "subsidized projects" and "independent projects". Both types of project are similar in terms of accompanying the grants from central governments. The difference is that the grants for "subsidized projects" are specific grants, on the other hand the grants for "independent projects" are general grants as a form of local shared tax, which contributes to the autonomy of the finance structure of local government.

Figure 1 displays recent increase in the independent project. In 1986, the amount of "subsidized projects" and "independent projects" were almost the same, but during the 1990s the growth rate of "independent projects" maintained a constant growth rate while, "subsidized projects" remained largely unchanged

The grants paid to local governments for bond issues play an important role in capital expenditure by cutting the burden of bond interest payments. Figure 2 shows how the cost of independent local public investment projects is financed. When local governments conduct such public projects aimed at promoting the development of the local area, they have to finance 75% of funds by issuing bonds and 25% by their own revenue. However, they receive subsidies from the central government amounting to 15% of total cost of its own revenue, and 30% to 50% of interest payments, depending on the local government's fiscal ability. This dramatically reduces the burden of conducting public project by local governments.

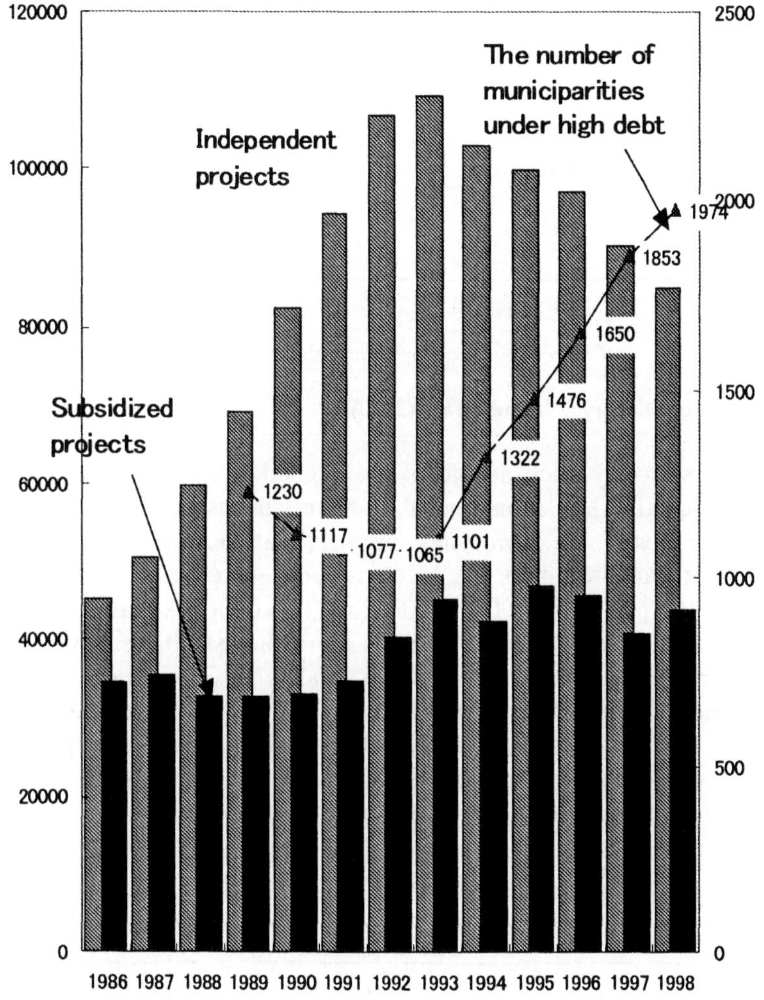

Figure1. The amount of public investment projects and the number of municipalities under high debt

Notes a) source Ministry of Home Affairs (2000)

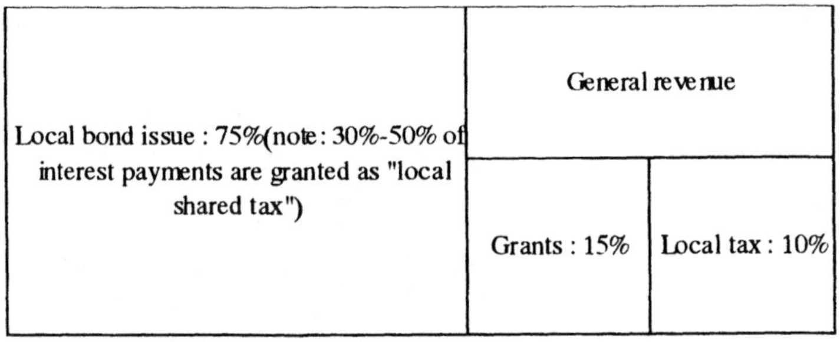

Figure 2. Finance funds in "Independent project"

Notes a) source Ministry of Home Affairs (2000)

The reason why such subsidies are needed is that there are more than 3200 municipalities in Japan and they have various sizes in population and fiscal capacities. Table 1 provides summary statistics for the population and fiscal ability according to the level of local governments. It shows wide variations in population, from 200 to 3,000,000(Yokohama city). Own-source revenues in local governments are rather small, especially in those with a small population or located in rural area. Some local governments cannot meet current expenditures out of current revenues and there is no room for interest payments, so the central government has to provide such subsidies for small municipalities. It also contributes to the central government policy that wants to encourage capital expenditures.

Table 1. Summary statistics for local governments

	Local tax ratio	Population
Mean	22.1	38,481
Median	17.6	10,879
Minimum	0.9	200
Maximum	75.2	3,301,232
99-%ile	63.3	462,338
95-%ile	53.6	145,607
90-%ile	46.1	72,378
75-%ile	31.2	26,376
25-%ile	9.6	5,725
10-%ile	5.8	3,160
05-%ile	4.5	2,047
01-%ile	2.9	865

Notes: The local tax ratio is the share of local taxes revenue on total budget.

In 1995, the subsidies included in fiscal demand amounted to 1400 billion yen, representing 6.5% of total grants. It is easily seen that the interest payment subsidy plays the major role in promoting project in local government's expenditure.

On the other hand, there is the rule limiting the debt which is issued by local government for financing capital expenditure. Local government debt is subject to a bond-debt ceiling. Whether bonds-debt financing reaches its ceiling or not, is measured by the ratio called "the bond limit ratio" which is the ratio of interest payments and standard fiscal scale.

The definition of its ratio is as follows

$$RTO = \frac{A-(B+C+E)}{D-(C+E)}$$

A: interest payment
B: special revenue used as interest payments
C: interest payments for the relief of the disaster.
D: standard fiscal scale.
E: interest payments that are included as standard fiscal need.

The bond-debt ceiling is the 3 years average of the ratio of general account resources for debt service. If it exceeds 15%, local government has to make a proper debt management plan and reduce the ratio to 13%. If it exceeds 20%, bond issuance for some kinds of capital expenditure is prohibited by central government.

If it exceeds 30%, almost all capital expenditures are prohibited except for measures to deal with natural calamities. It binds local government's activity. Because the ratio for debt service is the 3 years average, it moves slowly and may not respond to the break out of fiscal crisis quickly.

There are concerns about the bond limit ratio and the amount of bonds outstanding. It may not adequately display the financial condition of local government. Figure 3 shows the relationship between bond-debt and the bond limit ratio. As a whole, there is a positive relationship between bond-debt and the bond limit ratio. However, when the bond limit ratio goes upward and exceeds 10%, positive relationship becomes ambiguous, the bond-debt varies 5 times around 15%. It implies the local government in high debt can possibly have the same bond limit ratio with one in small debt. Even if its variation depends on the amount of independent projects conducted, it isn't appropriate to use it as an alarm for fiscal crisis.

Thus, in the next section, we investigate the relation of the bond limit ratio and the effect on capital expenditure.

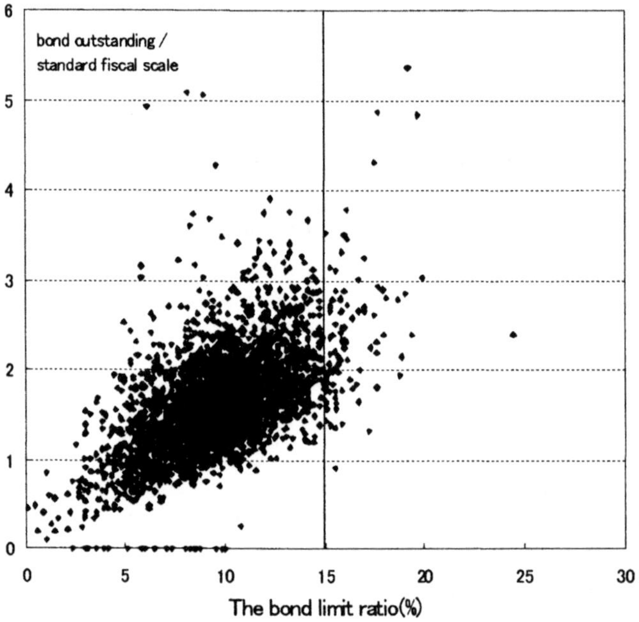

Figure 3. The bond limit ratio and local government bond

3. MODEL

In this section we present a simple two-period model, which takes into account the interaction between capital expenditures and the bond-debt ceilings. There are two kinds of local public expenditures, current operations and capital outlays (y). These expenditures are financed by local tax, subsidies (local share tax), or by issuing bonds. But bond financing is allowed only for capital outlays. The interest payment for bonds is conducted in two periods and is equal along the periods. So interest payment is denoted as R、which satisfies equation. $y = Ry + Ry/(1+r)$. So R can be calculated as $R = (1+r)/(2+r)$.

Assume that capital expenditures conducted by local governments bring about subsidies from the central government by m % per expenditures. The expenditure for period 1 is composed of the current operations (x_1), interest payments (Ry) and its sources of revenue are tax (t_1), and local shared tax as unconditional grants from central government. Local shared tax is widely used as a tool equalizing revenue capacity in Japan and is distributed according to a formula based upon the difference between standard fiscal needs and standard fiscal revenues. As a whole, standard fiscal need are composed of two kind of fiscal needs, operational expenditure and interest payments. However, standard fiscal needs are derived by a complicated formula that isn't easy to understand. In this case, it is assumed to be the sum of $\bar{t}$ which corresponds to operational expenditure and mRy, and standard fiscal revenue is equal to (t_1). So local shared tax is calculated as $(\bar{t} + mRy - t_2)$.

Local government budget in period 1 is summarized as follows

$$t + mRy = Ry + x + S \tag{1}$$

S is budget surplus. Local governments are not allowed to make deficits by law, and hence S must be above zero.

The budget of period 2 is undetermined, because it would change according to whether local government's bonds exceed its ceilings or not. It is determined by the value of the bond-outstanding limit. If interest payments in the second period exceed the amount determined beforehand, local government must cut off its expenditure.

The numerator of the bond limit ratio is the interest payment (Ry) minus project compensation (mRy), and the denominator is the standard fiscal scale minus subsidy. If the standard fiscal scale is assumed to be equal to the tax revenue (t_2), which is a probability value, it becomes also a probability value.

Denote α as the upper limit of bonds outstanding. If the bond limit ratio exceeds α, local government must cut off its expenditure as a penalty. So the condition local governments must keep is

$$\frac{(1-m)Ry}{t_2 - mRy} \leq \alpha \tag{2}$$

If equation (2) is not satisfied, local government must reduce its expenditure in period 2.

Denoting p as the probability that the ratio exceed α, p is defined as

$$p(y) = p[\frac{(1-m)Ry}{t_2 - mRy} \geq \alpha] \tag{3}$$

Increasing capital expenditures imply that the probability that the government breaks the ceiling rule will be higher. It is easy to see that the probability $p(y)$ becomes higher as y increases. Figure 4 indicates the relation between y and p. The x-axis is y, and the y-axis is p. A curved line in the figure is the cumulative distribution function.

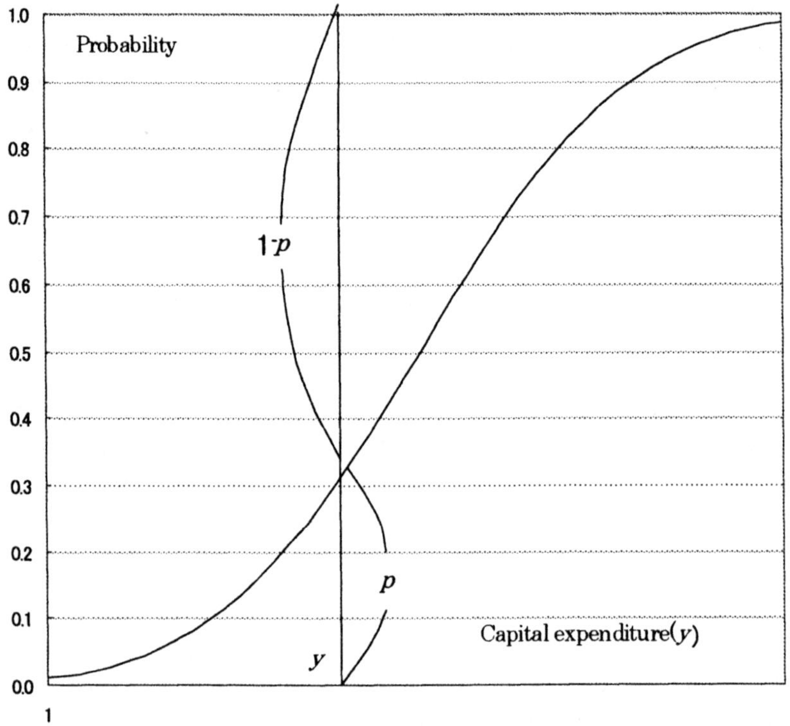

Figure 4. The relation of capital expenditure and the probability in breaking the ceiling

If local government increases public investment, y moves to the right, so probability that bond outstanding exceeds its ceilingincreases.

It is assumed that if local government breaks the rule, it must reduce γ $(0< \gamma <1)$ [1] units of x_2 per 1 unit. So local government must reduce its expenditure in period 2.

The revenue of the period 2 is the sum of local tax (t_2) and the local share tax. For simplicity, public investment outlay is done only in period 1 and standard fiscal need is assumed to be equal to $\bar{t}$ in both period 1 and period 2. Then local governmenfs budget constrainedcan be written

$$(1 + r)S + \bar{t} - \gamma x_2 = (1 - m)Ry + x_2$$

$$(1 + r)S + \bar{t} = (1 - m)Ry + \frac{x_2}{k} \tag{4}$$

Note that $k = 1/(1+\gamma)$, where k indicates the strength of penalty. If we combine the budget constraints in period 1 and period 2, by 2 cases, in which local government failed to satisfy the rule or not.

$$x_1 + (1-m)y + \frac{x_{2R}}{k(1+r)} = \bar{t} + \frac{\bar{t}}{1+r} \quad \text{with probability } p\ (y)$$

$$x_1 + (1-m)y + \frac{x_{2N}}{(1-R)} = \bar{t} + \frac{\bar{t}}{1+r} \quad \text{with probability 1- } p\ (y) \tag{5}$$

x_{2R} and x_{2N} indicate respectively consumption expenditure in 2 period in case breaking the rule and keep the rule.

The utility function of local government is assumed as

$$V = u(x_1, y) + \frac{u(x_2, y)}{1+\theta} \tag{6}$$

The local government maximizesits expected utility:

$$\max V = p(y)[u(x_1, y) + \frac{u(x_{2R}, y)}{1+\theta} + \lambda_R[\bar{t} + \frac{\bar{t}}{1+r} - x_1 - \frac{x_{2R}}{k(1+r)} - (1-m)y]]$$

$$+ (1 - y(P))\left[u(x_1, y) + \frac{u(x_{2N}, y)}{1+\theta} + \lambda_N[\bar{t} + \frac{\bar{t}}{1+r} - x_1 - x_1 - \frac{x_{2N}}{1+r} - (1-m)y]\right]$$

(7)

λ_R, λ_N are the co-state multipliers. In equation (7) the expectation is taken because local governments do not know if they may break the bond-debt restriction. The first order conditions are obtained by differentiating equation (7) on x_1, x_{2N}, x_{2R}, and y

$$\frac{\partial u(x_1, y)}{\partial x_1} = p\lambda_R + (1-p)\lambda_N \tag{8}$$

$$\frac{\partial_u (x_{2R}, y)}{\partial x_{2R}} = \frac{\lambda_R(1+\theta)}{k(1+r)} \tag{9}$$

$$\frac{\partial_u(x_{2N},y)}{\partial x_{2N}}=\frac{\lambda_N(1+\theta)}{1+r} \tag{10}$$

$$\frac{\partial u}{\partial y}+E\left[\frac{\partial u/\partial y}{1+\theta}\right]=(1+m)[p\lambda_R+(1-p)\lambda_N]+\frac{\partial p}{\partial y}\left[\frac{u(x_{2N},y)}{1+\theta}-\frac{u(x_{2R},y)}{1+\theta}\right]$$
$$=(1+m)\frac{\partial u(x_1,y)}{\partial x_1}+\frac{\partial p}{\partial y}\left[\frac{u(x_{2N},y)}{1+\theta}-\frac{u(x_{2R},y)}{1+\theta}\right] \tag{11}$$

From equations (8),(9),(10), it is easily seenthat

$$\frac{\partial u(x_1,y)}{\partial x_1}=\left(\frac{1+r}{1+\theta}\right)\left[kp\frac{\partial u(x_{2R},y)}{\partial x_{2R}}+(1-p)\frac{\partial u(x_{2N},y)}{\partial x_{2N}}\right] \tag{12}$$

Equation (12) shows that marginal utility of consumption in period 1 is equal to weighting average of tha in period 2. And also

$$\frac{\frac{\partial u}{\partial y}+E\left[\frac{\partial u/\partial y}{1+\theta}\right]-\frac{\partial p}{\partial y}\left[\frac{u(x_{2N},y)}{1+\theta}-\frac{u(x_{2R},y)}{1+\theta}\right]}{\partial u/\partial x_1}=1-m \tag{13}$$

Equation (13) shows that the marginal utility of substitution of y and x_1 is equal to 1-m which correspond to its relative price.

The public investment expenditure is the function of m. After all from equations (5), (11) and (12), the value of y, x_1, x_{2N}, x_{2R} is determined.

Hereafter, we assume the utility function is

$$u(x_i,y)=x_1^{1-\gamma}/(1-\gamma)+y^{1-\gamma}/(1-\gamma)$$

which γ is the parameter of relative risk aversion. And the consumption of period 1 is

$$x_1^{-\gamma}=\left(\frac{1+r}{1+\theta}\right)[kp(y)x_{2R}^{-\gamma}+(1-p(y)x_{2N}^{-\gamma}]$$
$$=\left(\frac{1+r}{1+\theta}\right)[kp(y)k^{-\gamma}x_{2N}^{-\gamma}+(1-p(y))x_{2N}^{-\gamma}] \tag{14}$$
$$=\left(\frac{1+r}{1+\theta}\right)[k^{1-\gamma}p(y)+(1-p(y))]x_{2N}^{-\gamma}$$

where we use the relation between x_{2R} and x_{2N} as a condition, that is $x_{2R} = kx_{2N}$

$$y^{-\gamma} + \frac{y^{-\gamma}}{1+\theta} = 1 - m + \frac{\partial p/\partial y}{(1+\theta)(1-\gamma)}[x_{2N}^{1-\gamma} - y_{2R}^{1-\gamma}]$$

$$(\frac{1+2\theta}{1+\theta})y^{-\gamma} = 1 - m + \frac{\partial p/\partial y}{(1+\theta)(1-\gamma)}[x_{2N}^{1-\gamma} - k^{1-\gamma}y_{2N}^{-\gamma}] \quad (15)$$

$$= 1 - m + \frac{\partial p/\partial y}{(1+\theta)(1-\gamma)}[1 - k^{1-\gamma}]x_{2N}^{1-\gamma}$$

Whether consumption in second period increases or not, depends on the degree of risk aversion of the local government. If the local government is risk averse, x_{2N} will increase.

Table 2 indicates how capital expenditure is decided in response to the variance coefficient of local tax revenue and subsidies. The variant coefficient is assumed to obeya normal distribution with mean as $(\bar{t}/2)$.

Table 2. Simulation results of preference for capital expenditure by local governments

subsidy m=20%				
Variation coefficient	0.75	1.00	1.25	1.50
Probability P(y)	0.035	0.048	0.062	0.077
Capital expenditure	1.255	1.150	1.063	0.988
Bond limit ratio	0.108	0.099	0.091	0.085
subsidy m=30%				
Variation coefficient	0.75	1.00	1.25	1.50
Probability P(y)	0.047	0.060	0.074	0.088
Capital expenditure	1.440	1.325	1.228	1.143
Bond limit ratio	0.111	0.101	0.094	0.087
subsidy m=40%				
Variation coefficient	0.75	1.00	1.25	1.50
Probability P(y)	0.061	0.073	0.086	0.100
Capital expenditure	1.665	1.540	1.430	1.335
Bond limit ratio	0.113	0.103	0.096	0.089

Capital expenditure is valued as the ratio of standard fiscal scale

k=. =0.5,. =0.05, r =0.1

Local government decides its expenditure by bond issue limits and subsidies. The degree of subsidy is determined so as to correct the fiscal ability of each local government. However, it is clear that it widens the relative price of consumption expenditure and investment expenditure and promotes local governmenfs capital expenditure.

Capital expenditure rises up from 1.255 to 1.665 in response to subsidies, which increase from 20% to 40%, and the probability of breaking the debt ceiling also rises from 3.5% to 6.1%.

This implies that the distribution of expenditure is not neutral to the volatility of local tax. Whether local government get a penalty or not, depends on the probability of local tax. For a local government, which gets high local tax revenue, revenue is also volatile.

4. BOND-DEBT CEILING AND CAPITAL EXPENDITURE BY LOCAL GOVERNMENT

In this section, we estimate the capital expenditure equation, especially autonomous capital expenditures. And we show the relationship between expenditure and the bond-debt ceiling.

There are several analyses about the preference of local government. For example, Holtz-Eakin, Rosen and Tilly (1994) find that state and local expenditure is determined primarily by current resources. In Japan, Shimizu, Doi, and Nakakazato (1999) show that the behavior of local government is very myopic. Our empirical equations relate the capital expenditure to various financial characteristics of the local governments.

Let Y_{it} denote the capital expenditure conducted by local government i during year t means time index. The estimation equation is as follows

$$\begin{aligned} \ln(Y_{i,t}) &= \beta_0 + \beta_1 \ln(Y_{i,t-1}) + \beta_2 RTO_{i,t-1} + \beta_3 (RTO_{i,t-1})^2 \\ &+ \beta_4 IDX_{i,t-1} + \beta_5 DET_{i,t-1} + \beta_6 OBG_{i,t-1} + \varepsilon_{i,t} \end{aligned} \tag{16}$$

IDX_{it} is fiscal ability index, DET_{it} is bond-debt outstanding, OBG_{it} is obligation expense. In estimation, we consider the non-linearity of the effect of bond-debt ceilings

The data is municipality's fiscal data in 1996, and 1997. We estimate the equation by OLS and GLS, in which we assume the variance of disturbance is proportional to the size of population.

Table 3 presents the results of two regressions of various local government traits on capital expenditure for this full sample of 3232 local governments. The bond-debt ceiling in the first order has the expected positive influence on public expenditures and the influence turns to negative in the second order. This means that the contribution of the bond-debt ceiling is decreasing according to its higher value.

In Figure 5, a curved line indicates the size of contribution. The X-axis is bond-debt ratio from 0% to 25% and the straight line is its marginal contribution. The curved line has peak around 7 or 8%, and decreases gradually. It changes to minus at 15% which is just the ceiling. It means the restriction of issuing debt becomes effective at the 15% level, and has no effect below 15%.

Table 3. Estimates of the capital expenditure by local governments

	OLS			GLS		
	coeffient	**t-value**	**p-value**	**coeffient**	**t-value**	**p-value**
Intercept	1.4579	10.838	0	2.1229	13.671	0
Capital expenditure(-1)	0.9724	83.31	0	0.9114	66.497	0
Bondlimit ratio	0.0289	2.382	0.035	0.031	2.644	0.021
Bond limit ratio	-0.0012	-1.952	0.075	-0.0017	-3.069	0.01
Fiscal ability index	0.159	4.154	0.001	0.333	6.446	0
Bond outstanding (second order)	-0.2274	12.199	0	-0.1705	-9.861	0
Obligation expenditures	-0.021	18.143	0	-0.021	-18.143	0
R	0.835			0.989		
RSS	530.654			2080.148		
df	3220			3220		

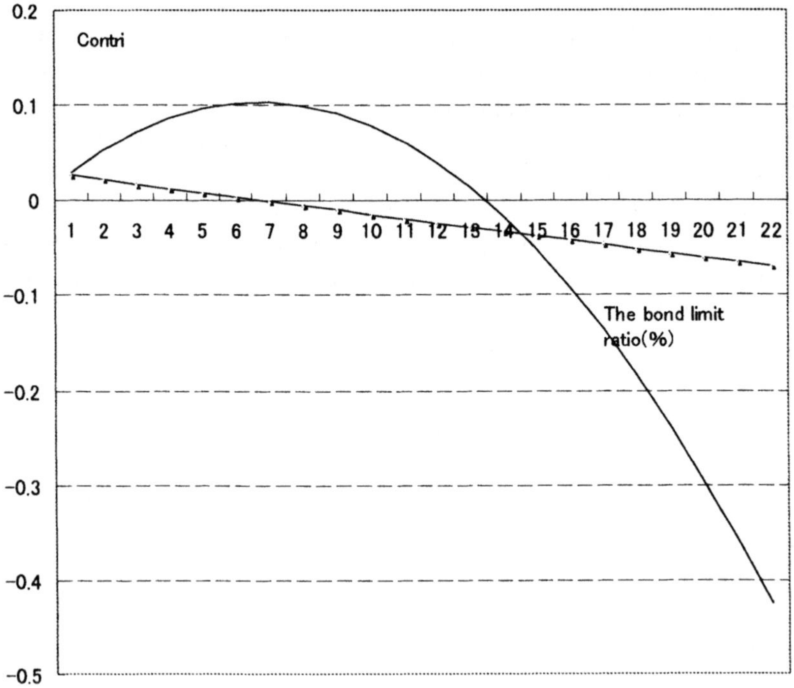

Figure 5. The contribution rate of the bond limit ratio on capital expenditure

5. CONCLUSION

This chapter documents a significant relationship between the bond limit ratio and capital expenditure by local governments. Comparing the benefit of subsidies they can get and the cost they would sustain in case of breaking restrictions, they decide the amount of public expenditures. Local government's preference for capital expenditures tends to vary according to the current codes and political rule. It changes the relative prices of capital expenditure and other expenditure and promotes capital expenditures.

The existence of a ceiling, which is common to every local government, also promotes this tendency. Because the probability in which local governments break the ceilings depends on how much own tax revenue they have. The local government with little tax revenue has more incentive to increase capital expenditure. In this chapter, we cannot demonstrate that this rule affects allocation efficiency. This study is left for the next research topic.

REFERENCES

Brueckner, J. K. and Joo Man-Soo, 1991, Voting with capitalization, *Regional Science and Urban Economics* 21, 453-467.

Doi, T., 1996, Flypaper effects in Japanese urban city finace, *Financial Review* 40, 95-119 (in Japanese).

Holtz-Eakin, D., H. S. Rosen and S. Tilly, 1994, Intertemporal analysis of state and local government spending: Theory and tests, *Journal of Urban Economics* 35, 159-74.

Ihori, T., 1996, kuni to chiho no buntansisutemu, *Financial Review* 40, 1-19 (in Japanese).

Ministry of Home Affairs, 2000, *White Paper forLlocal Governments in 2000* (in Japanese).

Shimizu T., T. Doi and T. Nakazato, 1999, The intertemporal allocation of local public expenditures, *Discussion Paper Series* J-82 Tokyo University (in Japanese).

Index

GPSR Compliance

The European Union's (EU) General Product Safety Regulation (GPSR) is a set of rules that requires consumer products to be safe and our obligations to ensure this.

If you have any concerns about our products, you can contact us on ProductSafety@springernature.com

In case Publisher is established outside the EU, the EU authorized representative is:

Springer Nature Customer Service Center GmbH
Europaplatz 3
69115 Heidelberg, Germany

Batch number: 10704043

Printed by Printforce, the Netherlands